Please return / renew by date shown. 22/8.
You can renew at: **norlink.norfolk.gov.uk**
or by telephone: **0344 800 8006**
Please have your library card & PIN ready.

23/03/15		

NORFOLK LIBRARY
AND INFORMATION SERVICE
NORFOLK ITEM

The Beginner's Guide to Wartime Collectables

Arthur Ward

Pen & Sword
MILITARY

First published in Great Britain in 2013 by
Pen & Sword Military
an imprint of
Pen & Sword Books Ltd
47 Church Street
Barnsley
South Yorkshire
S70 2AS

Copyright © Arthur Ward 2013

ISBN 978-1-84884-812-2

Typeset in 11pt Ehrhardt by
Mac Style, Bridlington, E. Yorkshire

Printed and bound in India by Replika Press Pvt. Ltd.

Pen & Sword Books Ltd incorporates the imprints of Pen & Sword Archaeology, Atlas, Aviation, Battleground, Discovery, Family History, History, Maritime, Military, Naval, Politics, Railways, Select, Social History, Transport, True Crime, and Claymore Press, Frontline Books, Leo Cooper, Praetorian Press, Remember When, Seaforth Publishing and Wharncliffe.

For a complete list of Pen & Sword titles please contact
PEN & SWORD BOOKS LIMITED
47 Church Street, Barnsley, South Yorkshire, S70 2AS, England
E-mail: enquiries@pen-and-sword.co.uk
Website: www.pen-and-sword.co.uk

Contents

Dedication

To the memory of the grandfather I never knew.

Horace Arthur Ward

February 2nd 1909 – November 14th 1940

Private, Buffs. Army No: 6284725

Army Form B.200E simply records 'Died (result of accident)'.

The 'accident' was the result of you being ordered against your free will to collect driftwood from a beach in Devon that you knew to be mined. Your violent death from a British anti-invasion weapon was made tragically ironic given your escape from advancing German forces during the retreat from France with the BEF only five months earlier.

From the wrong class, in the wrong place, at the wrong time.

But you are not forgotten and one year, 1940, became the touchstone for my interest in history and a conduit for my life-long fascination with military reliquary.

Acknowledgements

Lots of people have helped me in a variety of ways; either supplying precious artefacts, wearing them in photographs, lending advice or translating foreign documents. Thanks to everyone, especially the following:

Mirella Aslar, Keith Badman, Luca Bisoni, Martin Brayley, Penny Breia, David Carson, Jim Daly, Peter Donaldson, 'Taff' Gillinghmam, Paul Glennon, Fred Finel, Nick Hall, Gary Hancock, Dean Harvey, Phil Heycock, Jonathan Heyworth, Keith Homer, Richard Hunt, Duncan Hussey, Richard Ingram, Marek Kaszewski, Kent Battle of Britain Trust at Hawkinge, Graham Lancaster, Michael Larkin, Mike Llewellyn, Keith Major, Adrian Mathews, Glen Mallen, Stephen Maltby, Julian Money, Peter Osborne, Paul Phillips, Ron Shipley, Herb Schmitz, Nick Slee, Andy Smerdon, Roy Smith, Mick and Kath Sparkes, Bob Steadman, Darren Steed, Mark Taylor, Neil Thomas, Terry Voisey, Bob Whitaker, David Wickens, Colin Wright.

Introduction

Although warfare and military service is experienced by a relative few, its effects have a dramatic influence on all of us. Because the nature of armed struggle is so dramatic, it is not surprising that different elements of the milieu resonate with us in different ways. One component that continues to interest an enormous number of people concerns the regalia, arms and equipment of fighting men. 'Militaria' is the catch-all term used to describe the study and collection of authentic items of vintage and contemporary martial artefacts.

Overall layout of various British and Commonwealth badges, including: bronze cap badges for officers – Queen's Army Service Corps (WWI vintage, winning the 'Royal' prefix in 1921 and becoming the RASC); metal line infantry cap badges – Buffs, Royal Fusiliers, Suffolks, East Yorkshires, Black Watch, Volunteer Battalion Post Office Rifles; WWII plastic economy badges – Royal Artillery (bomb), Royal Engineers, Durham Light Infantry, King's Royal Rifle Corps, Devonshire Regiment; corps badges – Royal Artillery, Royal Engineers, RASC, REME, ATS; foreign and Commonwealth – Australian Commonwealth Military Forces, Free Dutch Volunteers (WWII); miscellaneous – Royal Marine Other Rank's helmet plate, RM Other Rank's cap badge, RN officer's beret badge and badge of the Palestine Police.

A broad-spectrum layout of military insignia awards and headdress, including: a WWII peaked cap belonging to a British staff colonel (note the red band); King's Royal Rifle Corp khaki beret of WWII period; British caps badges: a general's, Queen's Regt, Royal Scots, Manchesters, WWII Free Polish, RFC, German WWI Iron Cross 2nd Class, German belt buckle, Austro-Hungarian European medals and a WWI Prussian Pickelhaube helmet plate.

Naïve and primitive toy tank. Being handmade and not mass produced, it is all the more desirable and one can perhaps imagine a veteran of WWI fashioning this representation for an eager child. It probably dates from the early 1920s.

Collectors confer high values on all manner of original military paraphernalia. Some things such as badges, for example, have a more general appeal but serious buffs collect them with a passion equalled only by philatelists. Today, intense competition in the market for authentic twentieth-century military collectables has not only pushed prices higher as the supply for genuine items dwindles, but has generated a thriving market in quality replicas. These honest imitations *aren't* fakes and are especially prized by the growing band of re-enactors.

Fabric ARP badge worn on the overalls of men and women involved in air raid work.

Fought on two occasions (1880–1881 and 1899–1902) by the British Empire against the Dutch settlers of the independent Boer republics, the Boer wars introduced a century of remarkable change in warfare. As this Edwardian glass slide shows, gone were the scarlet tunics of the 'thin red line'. Khaki was king and soldiers fought as individuals, falling victim to sniper fire from rifles or being cut down with alacrity by the new machine gun – the deadly machine tool of the battlefield.

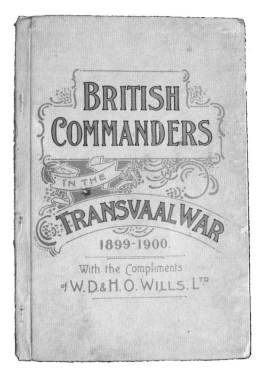

British Commanders in the Transvaal War. The First Boer War lasted from December 1880 until March 1881. This book deals with the British commanders of the Second Boer War fought from October 1899 to 31 May 1902, between the British Empire and the Afrikaans-speaking Dutch settlers of the Transvaal Republic and the Orange Free State.

It's not just about war fighting either. Collectors eagerly include non-military items such as those from the wartime civilian Home Front amongst their most prized possession.

Though warfare is characterized by violence and suffering, it also reveals some of mankind's more noble qualities such as bravery, camaraderie, compassion and even inventiveness. Things naturally develop rather quickly in an emergency. For example, the Second World War saw the introduction of the jet engine, cruise missiles in the shape of the German V, and even the first ballistic missiles when the 'doodlebug's' successor, the V2, was unleashed. There were new ideas in electronic early warning such as RADAR, ASDIC (known to the Americans as SONAR) and in computerized code-breaking such as ULTRA, the code name for the electronic decryption work going on at Bletchley Park that revealed the secrets of the German Enigma cipher.

One consequence of warfare impact on modern society is the intense interest in the study of military history as a subject, and films, novels and military biographies are perennial best-sellers. Many people, however, want to dig that bit deeper and get even closer to the subject, collecting the many artefacts that are uniquely associated with armed conflict. Sometimes these items are commonplace, such as badges and insignia, and sometimes they are much more unusual, such as the wooden rattles used by wardens to signify a gas attack or the brass bells they would ring to signify the end of such a frightening experience. Whatever the precise area of interest, collecting items can make the study of military history that bit more interesting. For many, handling and experiencing wartime collectables makes history tangible.

Although enthusiasts are unlikely to come across an affordable component from a Me 262 jet fighter, V-weapon or British Enigma machine, fortunately there are myriad other more accessible twentieth-century military collectables available. Items like badges, field manuals and small items of military equipment are affordable and easy to store. Those with deeper pockets and more space for storage can opt for larger items like helmets and

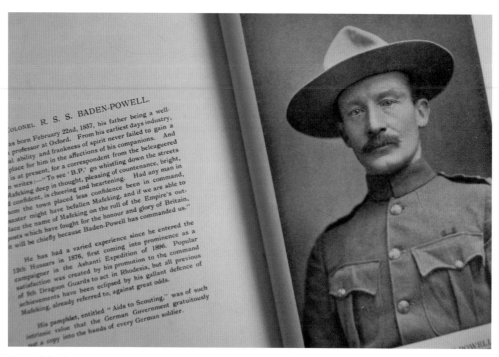

One of the famous British leaders depicted in *British Commanders in the Transvaal War*, Baden-Powell was garrison commander during the famous Boer War Siege of Mafeking, which lasted 217 days. Thanks largely to the cunning and inventiveness of Baden-Powell, although greatly outnumbered, the garrison held out until relieved.

uniforms, but as this book will explain, these present unique problems regarding display and conservation. Though perhaps more mundane, items from the Home Front – either those used by the numerous volunteer organizations such as the Home Guard and ARP or used in the home by families enduring the blackout and rationing – are also an important part of the story of total war and are still relatively plentiful. Whatever their original application, surviving authentic wartime relics tell a very special story. Furthermore, as is the nature of collectables, they are becoming scarcer with every passing year and so their financial value continues to rise.

Knowing what to look for, where to find things and what to pay for them are prerequisites for collecting success. For the novice such skills are essential. This book aims to demonstrate the wide range of collectables available. It goes into detail explaining the facts behind key objects and highlights such fundamentals as condition, how to detect fakes and, importantly, how to ensure your treasures stay in good shape.

Arthur Ward, Sussex, October 2012

Chapter 1

Insignia (Cloth and Metal)

Badge collecting has long been a popular pastime. Small, easy to store and relatively inexpensive, the myriad badges worn by soldiers, sailors and airmen have been a popular military collectable for generations. And badge collecting possesses a distinct virtue of enormous appeal to collectors as they don't take up too much space and can be displayed or transported with ease. A badge collection is unlikely to take over a house and get you in trouble with partners or parents because it has monopolized the home.

Badges are also pretty accessible. They are the sort of thing that can be found in most general collectors' centres, rather than one exclusively dealing with military collectables that include much larger and cumbersome items such as uniforms, edged weapons and headgear. They can often be found in the bits and pieces trays at car boot sales or in charity shops. And of course, they can now be readily bought off the internet via auction sites and specialized dealers. Because they are usually quite small, badges don't weigh very much and this therefore keeps postage costs to a minimum. The many virtues of badges make them a natural starting point for many a militaria collector.

Although regiments first began to be numbered long ago, insignia in the modern sense was not fully adopted by armies until well into the latter half of the eighteenth century. During this period in Britain, for example, the elaborate tarleton and peaked turbans worn began to be adorned with metal badges identifying differing units. Shakos, tall cylindrical

Cap badge of the King's Shropshire Light Infantry (KSLI), a regiment formed in 1881 but with antecedents dating back to 1755. In 1968 the KSLI was amalgamated with the King's Own Yorkshire Light Infantry, the Somerset and Cornwall Light Infantry and the Durham Light Infantry, becoming the Light Infantry. In February 2007 the Light Infantry itself became part of a new regiment, The Rifles.

Buffs helmet plate. The kind of insignia worn by British soldiers from 1881–1914.

Army badges might not be as cheap as they once were but they are still affordable. British Army insignia is at the core of my collection. Although at the time of writing (October 2012) the Army is contracting, with the *Daily Mail* saying: 'Cutbacks shrink the Army to smallest size since Crimean War…. The latest round of redundancies will see it shrink to about 97,000, its smallest size since the conflict in 1853. Its official strength in April last year was 101,300.' These dramatic cuts have resulted in a very few so-called 'super regiments' and made it a great time to collect the badges of the many, once proud regiments who have been amalgamated. It's a time to get them before they've gone, as they say. There is a finite supply of surviving Buffs, Highland Cyclist Battalion, Ox & Bucks Light Infantry and Connaught Rangers cap badges but with the imminence of the centenary commemorations of the First World War expect the existing supply to greatly diminish.

headdresses copied from the Austrians, who had in turn copied the design from Hungarian Magyars, were introduced in 1800. These 8-inch-tall 'stovepipes' featured large plates depicting unit insignia and were adorned with plumes denoting regular, light or grenadier companies. They quickly replaced the surviving mitres and tricorns. Headdress was supplemented by gorgets, a reminder of the days of armour. Officers wore these around the throat to denote regiment and rank and to indicate that the wearer was on duty. It was not until 1830 that gorgets ceased to be worn in the British Army. Pewter buttons featuring the particular numbers of individual regiments acted as an indication of service too. This period also saw the introduction of devices such as shoulder boards to identify rank. Previously status was only identifiable by the quality and cut of the uniform or type and prestige of weapons – either of which would have identified officer rank.

RAF King's Crown cap badge. Fortunately it is quite easy for even the novice collector to tell how old a badge is. The twentieth century quite neatly, well almost, divides in half between the time a male was on the throne and the reign of our current, female, monarch. King Edward VII ascended the throne in 1901 and Queen Elizabeth II succeeded her father, George VI, in 1952.

By the nineteenth century everything had become systemized to the extent that the concept of individual units being identified by name and number, and individual soldiery by standardized emblems of rank and arm of services, was internationally accepted. British armies were different from those of other nations in one important respect. Since Edward Cardwell's reforms of 1868 Britain was the only country that had concentrated on establishing very precise regional bonds rather

The Royal Fusiliers (City of London Regiment) cap badge. Worn on the racoon skin headdress adopted by fusilier regiments after 1901 (King's Crown, brass).

White metal badge of the Northumberland Fusiliers: 20th, 21st, 22nd and 29th battalions (Tyneside Scottish). WWI (1914–18).

Queen's Crown RAF cap badge. It pays to memorize the difference in design of each crown.

than just an association with a regimental number within the organization of its soldiery. Consequently, elaborate heraldic – often rather parochial – identities were adopted to denote provincial loyalties. Most other countries organized their military units solely based on less emotive and rather more impersonal numerical systems of unit classification.

In 1881, when the reforms of Secretary of State for War, Hugh Childers, came into effect, the numbering system for regiments was completely discontinued and county affiliations continued to be strengthened. Most of the single battalion regiments were combined into two-battalion regiments with, for the most part, county names in their titles. This created a force of sixty-nine Line Infantry regiments – forty-eight English, ten Scottish, eight Irish, and three Welsh. The British soon discovered that men fought with vigour if they were part of the Gloucesters, Wessex Regiment or East Kents and not simply identified as the '4th Regt of Infantry of the Line'. The 1880s also saw the British Army adopt cloth helmets that remained in service until 1914. Because the older shako plates were unsuitable and the recent reforms had encouraged territorial titles to replace regimental numbers, new eight-pointed helmet plates – forerunners of twentieth-century cap badges – were designed for the new headgear.

Despite all these introductions, as late as 1913, the Household Cavalry for example, was distinguished by its uniform and was without a cap badge. The issue of khaki uniforms to cavalry regiments that year made the provision of cap badges a necessity and so a bronze cap badge was issued to them too. Perhaps the most famous Secretary of State for War was Lord Haldane. His reforms of 1907–1908 saw the creation of the Imperial General Staff and under his direction the British Army accommodated the necessary changes in war-fighting forced upon it by the introduction of the quick-firing bolt-action rifle and the earliest automatic weapons. Combined with use of camouflage,

A broad selection of British WWII cloth insignia, including qualification, unit and field service emblems. Shown: parachute wings and 'parachute-trained' badge; tank crewman; machine gunner; motorcyclist; the crossed swords of a PTI (physical training instructor); 5th AA Division; printed 43 Wessex flash; grey and yellow embroidered Army Catering Corps field service strip and a set of three embroidered red infantry seniority strips.

Haldane's reforms encouraged the development of 'fire and movement' techniques and the introduction of lessons learned from Boer commandos during the South African War. Even the wide-brimmed slouch hats employed by the Afrikaans irregulars quickly found their place in British Army stores.

The introduction of khaki uniforms and shrapnel helmets necessitated the introduction of battle patches. With no insignia on helmets and shoulder titles being indistinguishable at distance, these cloth devices readily identified battalions or brigades within a division. They thus enabled commanders to make battlefield dispositions without the need to be present amongst the front-line fighting. For the first time, senior army officers could lead their men into battle from the secure locations far behind the front. While the British clung on to county designations, the armies of Germany and France had long used a more impersonal system of numbers to identify individual regiments. The Germans also employed a system of colour piping (*Waffenfarbe*) on collars and shoulder boards to denote arm of service. In Britain at the end of the First World War it was decided that the majority of the enormous variety of insignia that had crept back onto combat uniforms – some of it distinctly unofficial – should be removed to smarten things up and, literally, get soldiers wearing uniform outfits. Thus, the new British battledress pattern introduced in 1939 was designed with homogenous simplicity in mind.

The Queen's Royal Regiment cap badge featured the Lamb of God, which took away the sins of the world at Passover. Despite this, infantrymen in rival regiments rather disparagingly knew the West Surreys as the 'Mutton Lancers'! A proud regiment, formed in 1661, it was the senior English line infantry regiment of the British Army, behind only the Royal Scots in the British Army line infantry order of precedence. In 1959, it was amalgamated with the East Surrey Regiment to form the Queen's Royal Surrey Regiment.

US Insignia, including: cloth 17th Airborne Division (Rhine Crossing); 6th Armoured Division (17th & 6th, both of US manufacture); 9th Infantry Division (served in NW Europe and probably 'theatre made' in the UK); late, war corporal's stripe worn both on field and class A uniforms; group of three overseas service bars, each bar representing one year's service; US Army second lieutenant brass and captain's silver bars (typical of WWII period, with long bar pins used for attachment to uniforms

rather than the later short pins and clutch covers); enlisted soldier's collar disc for medical branch (example shown is of late war manufacture with short pin and clutch cover attachment; frosted gilt US officer's service cap badge (unusual, being produced in the UK by J.R. Gaunt).

This new uniform, inspired by both science fiction and the favoured choices of international tank crews then seen as the dashing twentieth-century cavalry, consisted of a stylish blouson and pleated, baggy trousers, and was designed to better suit soldiers for the new technological age. It was also considered an important aspect of field security that if a soldier was captured, this new uniform, sporting no markings other than slip-on shoulder boards that could be easily removed, wouldn't reveal his unit and therefore the dispositions of Allied troops. Black or green buttons were also introduced to replace the previous polished brass ones. Despite the designers' good intentions, by the end of 1940 the purpose and spirit of these new uniforms was somewhat undermined by the adoption of visible, coloured, field-service flashes. By 1941 this adornment had been augmented by the adoption of divisional, and in some cases, regimental, flashes. This development further undermined the purpose of the uniform. Indeed, by war's end, soldiers wore a wide range of insignia. Far from presenting a clean, almost non-descript, appearance, they were decorated like Christmas trees. Insignia denoting rank, regiment, division, trade, and qualifications (often produced in regimental colours, i.e. black on green for rifle regiments, black on red for King's Royal Rifle Corps, etc.) were supplemented by war service chevrons,

WWII period (King's Crown) Australian and Commonwealth Military Forces General Service cap badge. The famous 'Rising Sun' badge, it was worn on the brim of a slouch hat. This example is of the third pattern design and was worn in both WWI and WWII.

A selection of Third Reich insignia and ephemera including: tank crewman's skull cap badge; metal; Eagle swastika shield; national colours shield for Afrika Korps pith helmet; Feldgendarmarie (military police) gorget; RAD (Reichsarbeitsdienst – national labour service) brass door plaque; miniature booklet (*Battle in the East*), party armband and a rare standard top from an NSKOV flag. The National Socialist Kriegsopfer Verein was the Wehrmacht's old comrades association.

campaign ribbons and, in some cases, even regimental lanyards. The designers of the futuristically streamlined new battledress could only weep.

Twentieth-century wars also encouraged the development of often quite small units, now collectively known as Special Forces. These adopted specific cloth insignia to describe their role or capability. These units naturally depended on being able to distinguish themselves from the rank and file. They were the elite. In the British Army the most famous units within this

Formed in 1913, the Royal Irish Rifles had their name changed to the Royal Ulster Rifles in 1920. Their motto, '*Quis Separabit*', Latin for 'Who shall separate us', is very interesting. Despite the proclamation of the Irish Free State in 1921, The Rifles, who were identified with the North, continued to accept recruits from the rest of Ireland. Nearly half of the 1st Battalion serving in Korea in 1950 were Irish nationals. The regiment was disbanded in 1952.

This comprehensive selection of badges, many of them official and a good many unofficial and of the popular (and now very collectable) 'sweetheart' type brooch worn by spouses or off-duty National Service personnel, gives a pretty good idea of the number of organizations that sprouted up in defence of the realm. It also shows the choice of collectables available.

PORTSLADE-BY-SEA—SUSSEX EAST   FORM **A**

Evacuation of Mothers and Children

ADMIT TO TRAIN

Mrs. *L B Cuss*   Name   *44 Trafalgar Rd*   Home Address
Children *Brian Cuss.*   *Portslade by Sea*

Assemble at Recreation Ground Extension, Victoria Road, Portslade-by-Sea
58382

Britain's authorities assumed massive casualties would result from enemy air raids. Operation Pied Piper was the name given for the evacuation of children from Britain's cities and an order to 'Evacuate forthwith' was issued as early as 31 August 1939 (war was declared on 3 September). In the first four days of September 1939, nearly 3,000,000 people were moved to places of supposed safety in the countryside. Separated from their parents, schoolchildren were labelled like pieces of luggage.

relatively small cadre of fighting includes the Special Air Service (SAS), Long Range Desert Group (LRDG) and Special Boat Squadron (SBS). Some of these so-called 'private armies' sprang up following Churchill's order to the Special Operations Executive (SOE) to 'Set Europe Ablaze!' Collectors can never be sure if a regular army cap badge in their collection ever saw active service or left the United Kingdom. On the other hand, owners of Long Range Desert Group (LRDG) or Vietnam Special Forces insignia can be pretty sure that because so few were required and produced, those that *were* produåced were worn in the tactical theatre. Many smaller unit badges, generally cloth, were locally made so don't be put off by what looks like poor quality. Often operational units of the RAF, for example, were temporarily based at a desert airfield or advanced flying ground such as those hastily fabricated to support the build-up for the D-Day landings. These units often adopted unique regalia specific to their temporary disposition but because a

Selection of WWII British Army shoulder titles.

limited amount was produced they were all mostly worn in theatre, which adds to their provenance.

Nazi Germany burst upon the world stage in January 1933 with the dramatic and democratic appointment of Adolph Hitler as the country's new chancellor – his party having gained the largest share but not the majority vote in the earlier 1932 general elections. Nevertheless, it didn't take Hitler long to assume full power, adopt the title Führer, or 'leader', and change a whole range of established processes, procedures and organizational structures in an effort to consolidate power. Autocratic Fascism came to the fore and Germany bowed to the views of the one man who believed he could cure all the nation's ills and even erase the ignominy and humiliation many Germans felt after the punitive diktats of the 1919 Versailles Treaty. Interestingly, much of Nazi Germany's new way of doing things was modelled on the system of government introduced in Italy by Benito Mussolini in the 1920s. The Italian dictator was a charismatic leader who Hitler admired – or at

Brass King's Crown Royal Artillery cap badge.

Anodized 'Staybrite' cap badge of the Parachute Regiment. Post-1953 – Queen's Crown.

In 1922, the 17th Duke of Cambridge's Own Lancers and the 21st Empress of India's Lancers amalgamated to form the 17th/21st Lancers. This is a WWII-vintage white metal cap badge.

Royal Hampshire Regiment officer's silver-gilt and enamel peaked cap badge (post-WWI No. 1 dress badge).

least did during the earliest days of the Duce's hegemony. A key way Hitler consolidated his control over the German state was by stamping his authority on the armed forces. A veteran of the First World War, Hitler had been awarded the Iron Cross and was mentioned in despatches on several occasions. Although only achieving the rank of corporal during this conflict he felt he had a better facility for appreciating military matters than his generals – many of whom he despised, especially those who sprang from the Prussian elite and were of aristocratic descent. Hitler controlled his military machine by dispensing patronage, promoting those to whom he took a shine and approving funding for new types of weapons technology to keep his soldiers, sailors and airmen happy. Indeed, he equipped the air force and navy in direct contravention of the Versailles agreement and secretly trained a fledgling, and illegal, Luftwaffe in the Soviet Union and approved radical developments in tanks, U-boats and even battleships (though heavily-armed, new vessels like *Bismarck* were called 'pocket battleships' because their tonnage suggested they were not big enough to transgress the rules laid down by the victorious Allies at the end of the First World War). Naturally Hitler was keen to see that all this new equipment was served by fighting men dressed in appropriately modern and striking uniforms bedecked with brand-new regalia. Nazi reforms were wholesale, with uniforms, equipment and regalia all designed from scratch. The Führer's favourite iconography had its roots in an imagined Teutonic past of Aryan supremacy and knightly chivalry and the emblems of his armies were designed to echo this. Consequently, the armed forces became an inherent part in the full, theatrical, panoply of Hitler's new Reich.

As previously mentioned, colour had become an increasingly important part of German insignia since the turn of the twentieth century, with uniform piping (*Waffenfabe*) denoting arm-of-service, party affiliation, rank hierarchy and level of responsibility. Gold, for example, usually took precedence over silver. Hitler also managed to combine the Nazi Party's official emblem, the swastika, with the traditional German Eagle – effectively fusing the National Socialist German Workers' Party (NSDAP) and state. Therefore, individuals within Hitler's armed forces usually wore two principal badges: the Third Reich's interpretation of the national emblem – a swastika clutching an eagle in one of the various shapes to depict army, air force or navy – and an organizational emblem to describe arm-of-service. The badges and insignia of the Hitler's armed forces were a radical change from tradition and strikingly different from those used by other nations. Indeed so eye-catching and imaginative were they that, forgetting the often warped policies their wearers were ordered to pursue, collectors prize them above all others. Third Reich insignia united political, police and paramilitary organizations under the auspices of the Nazi Party. As a result, there were many badges and emblems available – one reason why

Anodized Scottish Highland Brigade badge with hackle, worn between 1959 and 1968. The motto '*Cuidich 'n Righ*' (Aid the King) first appeared on the Seaforth Highlanders' badge in 1881. On 1 July 1968, the Highland Brigade was united with the Lowland Brigade to form the Scottish Division. In 2006, the Scottish Division became a constituent in a single large regiment, the Royal Regiment of Scotland.

such insignia is still so collectable. The other reason for the popularity of Third Reich badges, especially, is their undeniable quality. Though many are of dubious provenance there is no denying their visual excellence. Well-established military artists and designers were involved in the creation of the new insignia. Chief amongst them was the Berlin-based artist and graphic designer Egon Jantke, who designed badges, medals and many uniforms for the Third Reich.

Ultra rare WWII German Army officer's (Obergruppenführer – upper group leader) collar tabs. As is mentioned in the text, authentic relics of the Third Reich command the highest prices.

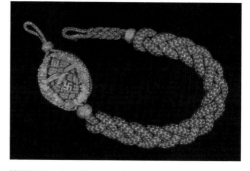

WWII Luftwaffe tunic lanyard denoting marksmanship.

Third Reich pin badges and insignia. From left to right: police arm patch for Berlin; selection of rally badges and party organization pins (including party membership badge; NSKK; Hitler Youth; BDM; Winterhilfe; German Red Cross; Frauenschaft, and a variety of sports organizations. In the box is a 25-year service medal.

Selection of WWII German Air Force (Luftwaffe) insignia with a very rare Luftwaffe dagger. Includes: breast Eagle's cloth and metal pilot badge; observer's badge; Other Rank's belt buckle; signaller's badge; and silver wire lanyard. The dagger features an amber (yellow) plastic hilt to match the Waffenfarbe of flying personnel and paratroops. It is shown with both belt hangers and silver wire knot. Daggers complete with hangers and knots command the highest prices.

A very old and rare badge belonging to the Lancashire Hussars Imperial Yeomanry.

A pretty rare badge belonging to the 4th Territorial Battalion of the Devonshire Regiment (1908–1921). Raised in August 1914 as part of the Devon & Cornwall Brigade, Wessex Division, they sailed for India in October, thereafter being stationed in Mesopotamia (the name for the area occupied today by Iraq, part of Syria and a small area of Turkey and Iran) for the rest of the war.

WWII Luftwaffe anti-aircraft gunner's badge featuring a depiction of the infamous '88'.

Design was one thing but the quality of their construction and manufacture is another reason for the popularity and durability of Nazi insignia. It is worth mentioning the names of the two most important manufacturers – especially as one of them, Wuppertal-based *Bandfabrik Ewald Vorsteher*, a name mostly reduced to the acronym 'BeVo' – is often featured on a badge's description. The other big manufacturer was Assman & Sons of Ludenscheid. If collectors come across either of these brand names on a piece of Second World War German insignia, they know they are on to a winner.

Together with British and Third Reich badges, the other big area for collectors is, of course, the badges and insignia of the United States. The history of US military insignia dates back to the eighteenth-century Continental Army fielded by General George Washington during the revolutionary wars. Washington's army could not afford to purchase uniforms but it was of course essential that his troops could tell friend from foe and identify the ranks of their superiors, and General Washington requested that badges be designed to help sort out this confusion. One development that endures to this day was the introduction of stars to distinguish the ranks of senior officers so that troops could tell a two-star major general from a one-star brigadier. During the time of famous battles at

The Artists Rifles cap badge. Raised in 1859 as part of a widespread movement to increase Britain's volunteer reserve in case of French invasion, this regiment was established by patriotic artists, including Frederic Leighton. The unit's first HQ was at Burlington House, the home of London's Royal Academy of Art. The badge was designed by William Wyon, who was the official chief engraver at the Royal Mint and, amongst other things like medals, was responsible for the earliest engravings of royalty (a very young Queen Victoria) on British postage stamps.

legendary names such as Concord, Lexington and Bunker Hill, these stars would be worn on the shoulder boards, or epaulettes. Interestingly, the US chevrons or 'stripes' as they are called in the British Army, were once quite similar, with both being worn point down. In both armies from approximately 1820 to 1903, chevrons were sewn on the sleeves of uniforms with the point facing down. For a couple of years American NCOs in various units wore them both up and down but in 1905 this confusion came to an end with Army Regulation No. 622, which stipulated that the points of the chevrons would be worn points upward. It also provided for the following colours to be adopted and formalized: Artillery – scarlet; Cavalry – yellow; Engineers – scarlet piped with orange; Hospital Corps – maroon piped with white; Infantry – light blue; Ordnance – black piped with scarlet; Post QM Sergeant – buff; Signal Corps – orange piped with white; West Point Band – light blue; West Point Detachment – buff. Allegedly the lozenge, or diamond shape, used in US armies to indicate first sergeant as a mark of distinction dates from heraldic devices worn by fighting men in the Middle Ages to indicate achievement.

Chevrons were used to designate the rank of officers through to the rank of captain as well as enlisted men. Captains, for example, wore one on each arm above the elbow; subalterns, on each arm below the elbow. They were manufactured from gold or silver lace, half-an-inch wide, and conformed in colour to the button of their regiment or corps.

Three skill-at-arms badges. Two denote a marksman (the red-backed example for wear on mess kit). The crossed SMLE is the badge of either a musketry instructor or weapons training instructor.

Very rare Local Defence Volunteer (LDV) brassard. Amongst the many things that grabbed Churchill's attention when he became prime minister in 1940 was the name of this new volunteer force. He didn't like it. So although it had been formed as recently as 14 May, despite the cost and inconvenience, on 22 July the LDV was officially renamed the Home Guard and the existing brassards were scrapped!

Sussex District, South-Eastern Command Home Guard battalion shoulder insignia.

US rank insignia grew in importance but the advent of the rifled musket in the Civil War encouraged enemy sharpshooters to target officers, who soon learned to remove their military rank insignia as they approached the front-line.

The US Army first wore battle patches in 1918 when the 81st Division began to sport them. Other units followed suit, using the patches and insignias to identify which unit they belonged to. Of the two principal kinds of patches, the one worn on the left shoulder signifies membership to a particular military unit while the patches worn on the right shoulder are reserved as a badge of honour and identify the wearer as having been under fire in the combat zone with a particular unit. The development of twentieth-century US cap badges can be traced back to the introduction of forage caps into the army in the nineteenth century. In 1902 the US Army introduced a new pattern of dress cap with a badge fixed to the front of the crown. Although initially produced in blue, in keeping with international practices this new hat was soon manufactured in khaki, with the blue service uniform being relegated to dress uniform purposes. The pattern of this cap is very similar to that worn by US troops today.

Known as Home Guard Auxiliaries (not to be confused with the clandestine Auxiliary Units, who also used the Home Guard for cover), in April 1943 women were 'officially' allowed to join the Home Guard, although in a non-combatant role. Although no uniform was issued they were given a plastic brooch badge. Not surprisingly, this is now pretty collectable and prices have soared.

Bi-metal cap badge of the Lincolnshire Regiment. Raised in 1685, the distinctive sphinx was added to the badge in 1801 to commemorate the regiment's actions against Napoleon in Egypt. After the Second World War it was honoured with the name Royal Lincolnshire Regiment. In 1960 it amalgamated with the Northamptonshire Regiment to form the 2nd East Anglian Regiment. Today, both regiments form part of the Royal Anglian Regiment.

Featuring the White Horse of Hanover (the regiment could trace its antecedents back to 1685), this is the bi-metal cap badge of the 3rd King's Own Hussars, which took its name in 1861. In 1936 the regiment swapped its horses for armoured cars but by the time it was in action at El Alamein it was equipped with tanks, where all but five of them were destroyed in the first days of the action.

Between 1911 and 1941 US armies wore another very distinctive type of hat, which again sported the unit's badge. This was the classic 'Montana peak', a kind of hat still worn by some organizations today – most notably the Royal Canadian Mounted Police.

There are two other iconic US Army hats of the twentieth century: the garrison cap, a development of the US First World War 'Overseas' cap featuring rank insignia and coloured piping to denote arm-of-service (i.e. red and white for engineers); and the

WWI British cloth insignia. The 'bomber's' qualification badge on the left was awarded to personnel trained to be most effective in the offensive use of the standard issue British hand grenade – the famous Mills bomb. To the right is an embroidered slip-on title denoting the Suffolk Regiment. An economy measure introduced to replace the existing brass shoulder titles and designed to be attached to shoulder epaulettes, it was not unknown for such insignia to be sewn directly to the top of a soldier's sleeve.

M1951 Ridgeway field cap, a development of the M1943 field service cap but stiffened up by the addition of cardboard inserts to smarten the US Army up during the Korean War (rear echelons being seen to adopt a sloppy 'field garrison' appearance as in the TV show MASH.). A development of this classic headgear was immortalized when included with first generation GI-Joe and Action Man figures.

Bi-metal Other Rank's cap badge of the Lancashire Fusiliers, worn until 1921. During WWI the Lancashire Fusiliers provided a total of four Pals battalions (1st, 2nd, 3rd and 4th Salford Pals). Pals battalions comprised men who had enlisted together and were told that they would be able to serve alongside their friends, neighbours and work colleagues. Shortly after the outbreak of the war in 1914, Edward George Villiers Stanley, 17th Earl of Derby, decided to form a battalion of men from Liverpool saying: 'This should be a battalion of pals, a battalion in which friends from the same office will fight shoulder to shoulder for the honour of Britain and the credit of Liverpool.'

The US armies were the fastest to move away from metal cap badges, which were usually national and collar insignia and which generally denoted unit affiliations. They instead adopted a plethora of cloth patches to describe the numerous units in their huge army. Simplicity is the key with all US heraldic devices. The designs of US Army patches, for example, are testament to the enduring skills of their creators. What could be simpler and more recognizable than the patch of the US First Infantry Division, a red numeral one embroidered on an olive, drab, irregular shield shape or that of the First US Army, a block capital black 'A' set on a divided white and red rectangle, or even the US Army engineers – a white castle on a red ground?

Today, collecting the numerous official and unofficial battle patches adopted by US soldiers, sailors and airmen in the recent conflicts in Iraq and Afghanistan has proved very popular. However, from 2005 the introduction of Army Regulation 670-1 'Wear and Appearance of Army Uniforms and Insignia', which states: 'This regulation prescribes the authorization for wear, composition, and classification of uniforms, and the occasions for wearing all personal (clothing bag issue), optional, and commonly worn organizational Army uniforms. It also prescribes the awards, insignia, and accoutrements authorized for wear on the uniform, and how these items are worn,'

Encouraged by Lord Derby's success, Kitchener promoted the idea of organizing similar recruitment campaigns throughout the entire country.

The Lancashire Fusiliers was amalgamated with other fusilier regiments in 1968 to form the Royal Regiment of Fusiliers.

played its part in regulating the proliferation of many bespoke and quite unofficial items.

Whilst not as varied a field perhaps as that of army badges, collecting the various insignia of the world's naval and air forces can be particularly rewarding.

The developments in Britain's air force during the twentieth century present collectors with a very interesting bounty, so dramatic were the changes to the structure

On 1 May 1936 the Royal Air Force amalgamated its separate flying training facilities at RAF Halton in Buckinghamshire, where Lord Trenchard had established the No. 1 School of Technical Training for RAF aircraft apprentices in 1919, with the established training facilities at Cranwell, the entry point for all those who wished to become permanent officers, which the RAF acquired from the Royal Naval Air Service in 1918. Training Command was the result. The rapid expansion forced by the exigencies of war, caused the RAF to reorganize things again in 1940 and Training Command was subdivided into Flying Training Command (headquartered at Shinfield Park, Berkshire) and Technical Training Command. This embroidered badge belongs to Peter Osborne and dates from 1952 when Peter joined the RAF on a Short Service Commission. He flew mostly Piston Provosts and then graduated to Gloster Meteors, Britain's first jet fighter. Peter remembers the badge cost five guineas, 'a lot of money when you are earning two guineas a week!' he said. The organization's Latin motto, '*Per Laborem ad Summa*', translates as 'Through toil to supremacy'.

of the organization in its earliest days. On 13 April 1912 King George V signed a royal warrant establishing the Royal Flying Corps and a month later the Air Battalion of the Royal Engineers became the Military Wing of the Royal Flying Corps. The Royal Flying Corps (RFC) was the air arm of the British Army during the First World War but when it amalgamated with the Royal Naval Air Service (RNAS) on 1 April 1918, the Royal Air Force, (RAF) a truly independent air arm, was born. Early cloth or metal RFC and RAF badges prove to be a particularly popular choice for many badge collectors.

For those of a maritime bent, the insignia of the short-lived RNAS are a particular find. Indeed the RNAS produced insignia unique to a variety of highly sought-after roles including petty officer mechanic, leading mechanic and air mechanic – both 1st and 2nd Class. Additionally, the existence of General Branch, Engine Branch and Artisan Branch – the three main operational divisions applicable to each of the rankings – created a wide range of insignia. Qualification badges existed for everything from aerial gun layer to wireless mechanic telegraphist.

The US Air Force defines a patch as 'a cloth depiction of an emblem that can be affixed to a uniform' and United States military aviators have worn them since the First World War. Originally such depictions were first painted solely onto aircraft but soon such designs were transferred to cloth or leather (patches) and sewn onto leather flight jackets and other uniform items. Since 1923, official regulations have been in place for USAF organizations to gain approval for their emblems. The Air Force Historical Research Agency (AFHRA) – the organization charged with maintaining USAF organizational history and heraldry – currently has more then 14,000 approved emblems on file. Some of the patches worn on the shoulders of airmen today originated during the early days of military aviation and are the same designs as the emblems that first adorned the cowlings of First World War biplanes.

These charming porcelain miniatures are actually broaches, fitted with pins so they can be worn. They were sold by the Hitlerjugend and Bund Deutscher Mädel (boys' and girls' associations, respectively) during Winterhilfswerk (winter help work), an annual charitable money-raising drive organized by the National Socialist People's Welfare department in aid of the poor. As the war progressed such initiatives were used to help collect warm clothing for troops on the Eastern Front.

Whilst we generally think of fighting men as wearing subdued utilitarian uniforms embellished with the bare minimum of insignia to enable them to be readily identified and to receive the necessary respect and acknowledgement from their peers (both junior and senior), even a cursory study of the wide range of rank and organizational insignia still worn by modern fighting men presents an interesting and colourful cavalcade!

Chapter 2

Uniforms

Reconstruction of a WWI British officer of the West Yorkshire Regiment. He is wearing the soft cap and tunic with 2nd lieutenant's rank insignia on the cuff. By 1916, front-line field officers began to wear their rank insignia on their epaulettes in order to be less apparent to the enemy. The officer depicted wears leather 'Sam Brown' field equipment, named after the British general, Sir Samuel Browne (1824–1901). Legend has it that Browne designed the belt after his left arm was severed during battle in India. The design is said to have helped stabilize the belt so that the sword could be drawn with one hand. Details of 1908 pattern webbing equipment can be seen as worn by the two soldiers to the rear.

A few years ago I decided it might be best to avoid spending my hard-earned cash on items that I wanted to collect but moths and other parasites simply wanted to eat. As a consequence I no longer collect uniforms. With hindsight this decision was my loss because if you know what to do, fabrics can be treated to deter the attention of hungry bugs. There a host of ways to protect and display military costumes and regalia and keep them safe from infestation as well as harmful damage by sunlight. I wish I still had some of the items shown in this book, which I sold because I was unaware of even the most basic conservation techniques.

Everyone knows that apart from some very specialized irregular units, most armies are comprised of individuals who have sacrificed their uniqueness in favour of homogeneity. As the famous maxim goes, 'To make the man you've got to break the man', and one way of achieving this is to make sure everyone wears the same clothes. With every soldier wearing standardized military uniform the cult of the individual is sacrificed in favour of the greater unit. Not only is smartness and esprit de corps generally the result, it also helps rival belligerents tell friend from foe!

During the two world wars of the twentieth century, Britain saw its usually small peacetime army increase exponentially. More soldiers, sailors and airmen demanded a massive

British 'Tommy' from one of the so-called 'Kitchener battalions' serving on the Somme during the ill-fated offensive of 1916. His khaki woollen service dress and long puttees are distinctly of the period. He wears a recently introduced protective helmet of manganese steel. The small khaki cotton haversack on his left side contains his smoke-hood respirator, or 'PH hood', which was itself replaced by the new box respirator. His leather – rather than webbing – field equipment identifies him as part of that army of volunteers who first took to the field in 1914.

increase in the production of uniforms and equipment and hundreds of new designs for regimental badges and divisional flashes. In the Second World War Britain was second only to the Soviet Union in the manner it galvanized its nation towards total war. Women assumed many of the peacetime roles previously occupied by men (in 1941 Britain was the first Western country to conscript women for service in the uniformed Auxiliary Services). Those men too old or unfit for military service enlisted in a variety of jobs in the ARP, the Home Guard, the Observer Corps and a host of other Civil Defence organizations. Other than a remaining rump of CD volunteers trained in nuclear, biological and chemical defence during the Cold War of the 1950s and 1960s, the other National Service organizations – the Women's Land Army, ARP, Fire Watchers, Auxiliary Firemen, First Aid Nursing Yeomanry and dozens of other groups who had given of their free time during the war – simply ceased to exist.

The Second World War saw the culmination of a period of intense change in the way different nations clothed their regular forces and auxiliaries. Change had started at the beginning of the century when new, more accurate weapons with a longer range determined that it might be better to opt for at least partial concealment rather than parade

Three members of the Royal Sussex Regiment, in early pattern battledress, manning an early pattern Vickers gun. This weapon was water-cooled (hence the rubber hose and can for condensing water). It fired .303 calibre belt-fed ammunition, which was carried in the accompanying leather-handled ammunition box. The soldier on the right has a shoulder-slung leather case for the dial sight used for indirect fire. This is the more desirable Vickers machine gun because, being of the fluted jacket variety, it is most associated with WWI. Later versions were smooth-jacketed. Surviving deactivated weapons on the international collectors' market are mostly Australian, this country having held on longest to its wartime stocks.

opposing forces opposite each other in brightly coloured attire (only necessary because the days of black powder meant that battlefields soon became enveloped in a thick fog of gun smoke and commanders needed to be able to identify their units amidst the mire). The twentieth century saw the real beginnings of practical, fully functioning uniforms for fighting men. Dun-coloured or khaki cloth was the colour of choice for the British and field grey was favoured by the Germans.

The furious revolution in battlefield technology not only enabled armies to kill with accuracy over greater ranges than ever before but both small arms and larger calibre field pieces fired faster and could be reloaded with far greater rapidity than previous models. The machine gun – the power tool of the battlefield – exacerbated the need for change. New technology made the

Three Battle of Britain period RAF pilots in a variety of iconic outfits. These include an early pattern Sidcott suit, officer's service dress and Irvin sheepskin flying jacket. Both 'Mae West' life preservers are of the early pattern. One has been painted with high visibility yellow dope, as used on RAF training aircraft such as Tiger Moths and Harvards. The officer in service dress wears the Luxor type goggles and the chap in the Irvin jacket wears Mk III(a) goggles. Leather flying boots of 1936 and 1393 pattern are also shown. The flyer in the Sidcott suit has a set type parachute as worn by fighter pilots.

battlefield an even more dangerous place than it had ever been. The days of rival armies lining up and facing each other in serried ranks had gone. If they could, soldiers needed to blend in to the local surroundings and be as indistinct as possible. Camouflage and drab uniforms were *de rigueur*.

Copying the practices of the Afghan tribes they had encountered on the North Western Frontier, British troops first changed their uniforms from bright scarlet to khaki (Persian for 'dust') during the Abyssinian Campaign of 1867–1868. It was from the time of the Second Boer War (1899–1902), when a darker shade of khaki serge was adopted and also used for home service, that the colour with which we are familiar to this day became firmly adopted. Interestingly, the German Army also adopted a drab colour – field grey, which also went some way towards obscuring troops on the battlefield. Curiously, French uniforms remained bright blue and edged with crimson until well into the twentieth century.

Britain's involvement with the First World War is generally characterized by military failure with soldiers deployed as so many chess pieces upon a lethal game board – lions led by donkeys. Whilst there's no doubt that the Imperial General Staff repeatedly messed things up (with fatal consequences for the unsuspecting conscripts packed into shell-torn trenches), the powers that be did get some things right. The British Army was the only participating belligerent

British private soldier in late 1940 wearing 'un-blancoed' 1937 pattern webbing and carrying a MkV respirator haversack (worn at the alert). Across the top of his small pack his 'Cape Anti Gas' is worn rolled. The bolt of his Lee-Enfield rifle is open and awaiting the magazine to be charged with two clips, each of five rounds.

First pattern British Army WWII battledress blouse badged to a lieutenant colonel in the Worcestershire Home Guard. Note the unlined collar of the blouse and the plain khaki pips and crowns with coloured backing worn by the Army early in the war and continued by the Home Guard thereafter. The medal ribbon denotes the 1939/45 stars. Introduced in 1943, this campaign ribbon suggests the officer had already seen some regular army service. Also shown with the blouse is this officer's khaki barathea and coloured field service caps (Worcestershire Regiment).

'Let them all come!' A Local Defence Volunteer scans the horizon from his vantage point near Beachy Head in Sussex.

completely dressed in what was, in effect, camouflage. In 1925 Britain's official historian, First World War Royal Engineers officer James Edward Edmonds, wrote: 'The British Army of 1914 was the best trained, best equipped and best organized British Army ever sent to war.' It's a tragedy that it was deployed with the same skill as it was armed and clothed.

The French Army that advanced to meet the Germans in 1914 wore a uniform that had changed little from the days of the Franco-Prussian War in 1870. French infantrymen still wore the traditional red kepi and trousers with a conspicuous blue greatcoat on top. They carried a heavy pack and their *Fusil Modèle* 1886, the Lebel 8mm rifle, sported a long and unwieldy bayonet.

At first, many soldiers in the German and Austro-Hungarian armies who faced the Anglo-French armies on the Western Front wore helmets and knee-high marching boots that harked back to Prussian military tradition. But the M1895 *Pickelhaube* was the last in a series of spiked helmets made of boiled leather with spikes and fittings made from brass. These gave scant protection and in the field were worn with a cloth helmet cover with the regimental number in red on the front. In 1916 it was replaced by a steel helmet, the M1916 *Stahlhelm*, which protected the face, ears and neck and was superior to Allied headgear. The field grey German M1907/10 tunic, with its detachable shoulder straps piped in colours identifying individual army corps, was also replaced with a new tunic, M1915 *Bluse*, as well as a new greatcoat. The M1895 belt was made of tan leather and buckle plates varied according to where in Germany individual regiments came from. The six brown leather M1909 cartridge pouches worn on the belt each held four five-round clips of 7.92mm ammo for the soldier's *Mauser Gewehr* 98 rifle.

The German Army soon found that its uniform and equipment needed to be changed to adapt to the unforeseen operational restrictions of life in the trenches. So in September 1915 there were a number of modifications such as the blackening of leather equipment

Three Luftwaffe aircrew members, including an officer and NCO. In the centre a bomber crewman wears standard flying overalls, kapok life preserver, parachute and summer finish flying helmet. To the left the senior NCO (an observer) wears an Other Rank's (OR's) tunic (as opposed to the *Fliegerbluse*), breeches and cap with white summer cover. The officer on the right (an Oberstlieutnant, or lieutenant colonel) is wearing the *Fliegerbluse* and breeches in officer quality cloth. He wears the corresponding officer quality *Feldmütze*, with silver wire piping and insignia. Interestingly, the officer (a fighter pilot) wears the inflatable life jacket, as worn by fighter crews. Note the flare cartridges strapped to the bomber crewman's boots.

Iconic image of a British infantryman clad in early pattern battledress amongst the dunes of Dunkirk in May 1940. He has only his trusty .303 Lee-Enfield service rifle with which to hit back at marauding Stuka dive-bombers.

Luftwaffe flying clothing: kapok life jacket, canvas flying helmet, rubber oxygen mask with hose, flying goggles and the black leather blouson-style flying jacket, which was often privately purchased.

and painting the new steel helmet in camouflage patterns of dull red-browns, ochres and greens divided by black lines. Like most armies, the Germans also eventually introduced protective body armour worn by men in exposed positions such as sentries and machine gunners.

Although the British Army's khaki was a form of camouflage and dated back to the eighteenth century, when Prussian Jaegers had worn green uniforms for concealment – as the British Rifle Brigade did some years later during the Napoleonic Wars – the first truly modern 'disruptive' camouflage was introduced by German armed forces during the inter-war years. *Buntfarbenaufdruck* (multi-coloured colour print) was introduced as early as 1931 and worn by the nation's territorial defence force, or Reichswehr. The *Zeltbahn 31* shelter quarter was issued to all units of the and as well as the tiny Reichsmarine (territorial navy). With the ascendency of Hitler, in 1935 the Reichswehr became the Wehrmacht and the *Buntfarbenaufdruck* was renamed *Heeressplittermuster 31* (army splinter pattern M1931). All units in the Heer (army), Kriegsmarine (navy) and Luftwaffe (air force), wore this disruptive material until 1945.

After the First World War Britain also recognized that a new uniform, not just a new colour, was needed. The British threw out the old-style service dress that in one form or another had served its soldiers well since the end of the nineteenth century and it wasn't until 1939, when the Second World War broke out, that this new battledress was ready. Its design was very modern and followed many of the principals established by students of the modern battlefield, like Liddell Hart and Fuller. It was also quite fashionable with the blouson and baggy pants combination, in keeping with the style of garment chosen

Irvin sheepskin flying jacket worn by RAF aircrew during WWII. Designed by American aviator Leslie Leroy Irvin, the iconic jacket wasn't his only claim to fame because he was also the inventor of the rip-cord system for parachutes. In 1919 he was the first man to make a free-fall jump from an aeroplane. Early versions of Irvin's jacket came with symmetrical back panels, while some later jackets were constructed from smaller, irregular offcuts. Originally conceived as a suit with matching sheepskin trousers, of which there was an electrically heated version, the jacket alone is most typically thought of as being worn over service dress, or even battledress, by fighter pilots. This is a very rare example of a classic piece of RAF flying equipment, dated 1941. To ensure authenticity look for zip fastenings marked 'AM' for 'Air Ministry'.

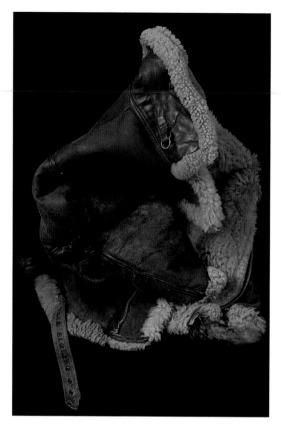

by adventurers and downhill skiers during the 1930s. It is often erroneously referred to as '1937 Pattern'. In fact, it originated in 1938 but didn't enter service until 1939. One reason for the confusion perhaps is that the new web equipment designed for it dates from 1937 and is known as 37 Pattern. This revolutionary arrangement of belts, braces and pouches designed to distribute weight across a soldier's upper body more evenly than the previous 1908 Pattern worn by Tommies in the Flanders fields, was relatively complex to produce, so upon the outbreak of war, many soldiers wore the brand new battledress with the less satisfactory 1908 Pattern webbing. Despite the futuristic cut of British battledress, when it entered service in 1940 it was still manufactured from thick serge and wool was not the most

WWII USAAF bomber crewman in full flying rig. He wears the B3 sheepskin flying jacket, leather flying helmet, B7 goggles and A10 oxygen mask. Also noteworthy is the first field dressing (FFD) in rubberized cotton cover with two tie tapes that fix to the harness of his Type AN6513-1A parachute.

practical material either on a hot, dry battlefield or on a damp and muddy one.

Regardless of Britain's revolutionary change from a traditional and somewhat baggy service dress to the much neater battledress, most observers of Second World War military garb agree that the most practical and visually impressive actually belonged to the armies of Hitler's Third Reich. Just because a collector appreciates the design and manufacturing quality of a Third Reich uniform doesn't mean he or she has any sympathy with the many awful activities of Hitler's regime. But it is worth bearing in mind that many uninitiated observers might suspect otherwise. Certainly German Second World War uniforms were the first to provide what is generally considered a truly modern, integrated combination of camouflage and fabric finishes made the outfits versatile across a range of different tactical theatres and environments. In 1939–40, Hitler's Waffen (armed) SS could don *Zeltbahns* (individual ponchos that could be joined together to construct field tents) printed with a quite modern disruptive pattern designed to blend in with the surrounding flora and fauna.

A German Army officer of the Third Reich period wearing his dress tunic with its full ceremonial accessories, silver wire and black dress belt with corresponding round buckle, and silver wire braided lanyard. These uniforms were privately tailored for the individual officer. The white piping on his *Shirmutz* (peaked cap), shoulder boards and collar *Litzen* denotes that he is serving in the infantry. He holds the rank of Oberleutnant as evidenced by the single star on a flat silver board.

A WWII German Army infantry lieutenant inspects an NCO and two private soldiers. All are dressed in early pattern, 1940/41 vintage uniforms. The private soldiers wear *Feldmütze* and their tunics are early pattern M36 models with dark green collars. All soldiers still wear jackboots, unlike troops later in the war when ankle boots and gaiters were adopted instead. Also seen, representative of the Blitzkreig era, are cotton bags containing gas protective clothing attached to each respirator strap. Brown leather field equipment as worn by the officer is also typical of the early-war period.

One distinct advantage the Nazi Party had over the existing military structures of its rivals was that to a large degree it was new. The election of Hitler and his cronies in 1933 swept away not only traditional military hierarchies, but condemned a great deal of existing military thinking to the dustbin as well. Certainly, in Hitler's eyes such bourgeoisie principals had led to the stalemate and bloody frustration of trench warfare. He had witnessed it at first hand and was determined that his new army, initially largely built on bluff and histrionics, would be a modern force on the battlefield. *Blitzkrieg* (lightening war), which so nonplussed the Allies from the invasion of Poland to the fall of France, was evidence of these new principals in practice. Not only did the Third Reich throw away most of the outdated principals of its predecessors and adopt new theories to guide its armies in battle, it also developed a new system of dress designed to complement the pace demanded by the principals of *Blitzkrieg.*

Hitler's armies spent much of the war relying on the horse as a prime mover for supplies and artillery – even though deficiencies of command would condemn hundreds of thousands of ill-equipped soldiers to a frozen death in Russia on the whole his designers provided the troops with a more practical uniform than that of other armies. Certainly, when compared to the often ill-fitting garb of British and Commonwealth soldiers clad in the new 1939 battledress for which its designers had such high hopes, the Wehrmacht fighting men were in a different league as far as fit and utility of their uniforms were concerned. Indeed it could be argued that although often used to such malignant ends, German Special Forces – be they Waffen SS or Fallschirmjäger – pioneered some of the most advanced uniforms for their day ever seen on the battlefield.

The Allies watched German developments in military tactics and equipment closely. Prime Minister Winston Churchill encouraged the creation of a British parachute division after hearing accounts of Nazi Fallschirmjägers breaching the Belgium fort at Eban Emael, which had for so long been thought to be invulnerable. Thus a significant development in the design of the kind of uniforms with which we are still familiar today was actually inspired by the requirements of the Special Forces or irregular troops. Very soon, Hitler's supposedly invulnerable Fallschirmjägers were wearing innovative camouflaged smocks.

The German style of uniform might have been widely adopted by other belligerents but, ironically, after German troops dropped on Crete in 1941 and suffered losses of around twenty-five per cent or their total, Hitler decided that unsupported paratroops offered little potential on the battlefield a fact the Allies learned for themselves, the hard way, three years later at Arnhem.

As British and Americans quickly developed their own airborne forces they provided them with specialist uniforms that were very similar to those originated in Nazi Germany. Britain arguably went one step better. Its famous Parachute Regiment wore a classic – the Denison smock. This new smock replaced an expedient first-issue khaki-drill paratroop jump-jacket that had been directly copied in 1940 from the German

Very rare battledress denims. Used by soldiers for fatigue duties around the barracks, they were actually adopted by members of the ultra-secret GHQ Auxiliary Units as their uniform of choice. Thick woollen serge wasn't much use when you were crawling around an isolated underground bunker (OB, or Operational Base) or going about your nefarious business in woodland long after dark. Battledress denims were also the preferred choice of outfit for garage mechanics and industrial workers who snapped up the remaining surplus soon after the war ended. Hence their scarcity today!

Fallschirmjäger Knochensack. The new Denison smock was something else. Introduced in 1942, the 'Airborne Smock Denison Camouflage' sported a camouflage pattern designed by a Major Denison, a member of the camouflage unit working under the command of English artist and stage designer Oliver Messel. An alternative name was the 'Smock Denison Airborne Troops'. The smock was cut to generous proportions as it had to fit over the wearer's normal battledress. Of a sand base with a mid-green and brown disruptor in a brushstroke pattern, the smock was first employed by British Special Forces, most notably those within the Special Operations Executive (SOE). The economy version, introduced in 1944, dispensed with knitted cuffs and introduced a greener base colour more suitable for operations in Europe. This pattern was made famous by British and Polish troops engaged on the ill-fated Arnhem operation in September 1944.

The introduction of capacious cargo pockets on US paratrooper combat trousers in 1942 was the next major uniform change on the road to what we now consider modern combat kit. Although British battledress trousers featured pockets, they were in reality of little use. Until the middle of the war and the introduction of ankle boots, German

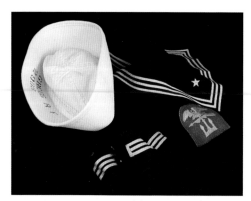

WWII US Navy rating's 'Blue Top' with navy Combined Operations patch on left sleeve (note the stars and stripes motif on collar rear), complete with sailor's white cotton gob hat, devised as a working dress hat but most commonly worn by US sailors at other times rather than the stiff blue 'Donald Duck' traditional sailor's cap.

WWII Navy gunnery rate at action stations. He is wearing a Mk II helmet, anti-flash hood and gloves, one-piece blue working overalls and money belt. His box respirator is of the long-hosed variety and therefore slung to his left side at the alert position with a special belt-type waistband securing the haversack to the body.

trousers tailored neatly enough so they could be tucked into knee-length 'jackboots' were even less generous.

Nazi and US uniforms also completed the next significant development in uniform design – the move to cotton and synthetics away from wool. Interestingly, the Third Reich was forced by expedience – the lack of natural resources and dwindling imports from overseas possessions – to adopt artificial materials. Prior to the Nazi invasion of Poland in 1939, the best quality German field blouses comprised an eighty-five per cent wool to fifteen per cent viscose/rayon mix. As the war progressed the viscose/rayon content increased, ultimately reaching a fifteen per cent wool to eighty-five per cent viscose/rayon (and recycled fibre material) as early as 1942. The later-war German uniforms were greatly inferior to those manufactured prior to the Battle of France in 1940. Fortunately, cellulose fibre (rayon, viscose rayon and acetate) production was facilitated by Germany's abundance of trees – the natural polymer cellulose being essential to plant growth – so the Germans knew that they could synthetically manufacture any fabric, silk, cotton or wool with this material and did not have to worry about sourcing raw supplies. One of the most commonly produced polymers, nylon was first produced on 28 February 1935, by Wallace Carothers at US chemical giant DuPont's research facility. Nylon was useful not just for stockings but also as a

Rare Wehrmacht WWII-period *Zeltbahn* found in Normandy and a likely relic from the fighting surrounding the choked bridgehead there. It is finished in what is referred to as 'splinter pattern' camouflage. Such use of camouflage and camouflage-patterned uniform by German special forces was more innovative than that of the Allied forces during the war. This clever garment doubled as a camouflaged, waterproofed poncho as well as a tent section – any number of which from three upwards could be linked to construct a suitable bivouac. German soldiers carried pole sections to complete the construction of such tents, which were ideally assembled from four *Zeltbahn* sections.

replacement for the silk used in parachute canopies. In fact, after this new material was used in military parachutes it was realized that, unlike silk, the previous staple material of such escape devices, nylon didn't develop static in the same way. It was found – too late for many unfortunate parachutists and pilots who died as a result of 'Roman Candling' when their canopies failed to open fully – that nylon parachutes exhibited none of the potentially fatal tendencies of silk. The discovery of this benign property of nylon was especially important to RAF fighter pilots, who were equipped with parachutes on which they sat during each sortie, unwittingly generating static electricity as they moved in their seat. Unused parachutes could be returned to the stores many times before a routine check. If a 'Roman Candle' resulted when such 'chutes were deployed, it was realized that the static generated within the folded silken canopy had the effect of causing the fabric to stick together rather than billow into a reassuring and supportive hemisphere.

It's not just because they are often better designed than British outfits that collectors and re-enactors prefer German and American uniforms. Another reason is that they are generally manufactured from material that is easier to clean and maintain. Cotton or synthetic uniforms are not only easy to keep fresh, they are also easy to reproduce, providing excellent bases for screen-printing camouflage patterns and readily acceptable of insignia such as cloth badges and patches. Furthermore, unlike the woollen battledress of British and Commonwealth troops, German and American uniforms aren't susceptible to parasites like moths or the dreaded 'woolly bears' that have feasted on many a treasured collection (but more about conservation towards the end of this book).

After the Second World War the British quickly introduced some new uniforms, particularly for forces serving in the Far East, where troops were issued with a new tropical uniform based on that worn by US marines in the Pacific. Unlike their American counterparts, British troops operating in this theatre wore uniforms manufactured from cotton drill as opposed to Aertex. This new uniform didn't entirely mimic that of the US and British squaddies still wore trousers cut to the existing battledress pattern rather than the more capacious cargo pantstyle of GIs. The old battledress endured until the late 1960s and was even worn during the Korean War in the 1950s, where it was either too cold in winter or too hot in summer. It was then fully replaced by Pattern 1960 DPM (Disruptive Pattern Material) uniforms.

With a divided Germany in the 1950s, West German troops still used two versions of the wartime German splinter – a four-colour pattern, *BV-Splittermuster*. But from 1961 until 1990 they wore olive green battledress based on the American pattern. A new type of disruptive camouflage, the five-colour *Flecktarn* pattern of dots and blotches, was chosen in 1976 and issued from the mid-1980s, but German reserve forces remained in the old olive-green uniform as late as 1994.

Full-length depiction of a post-1942 Sussex Home Guardsman patrolling atop Sussex downland. He wears equipment that includes pouches and cross-straps particular to the HG, designed to carry the large magazines for the Browning Automatic Rifle (BAR). The Model 1903 Belt Home Guard is also featured. His water bottle is carried in a leather cradle with strap and his anklets are leather rather than the webbing variety used by the regular army. Over his right shoulder he carries a 'lend-lease' American P17 rifle.

The Vietnam War witnessed more changes to American service uniforms during any time since the Second World War. At first, surplus sateen uniforms that had been first issued to troops for summer operations during the Korean War were issued to troops having to cope with the unfamiliar tropical heat of the Vietnamese jungles and forests. In 1965 looser and more practical uniforms manufactured from poplin were introduced. (Poplin, also called tabinet, is a strong fabric with crosswise ribs, giving a corded surface. Sateen, as its name suggests, is smoother, more akin to satin.) The new US materials were tough; the fabric was 'rip-stop', essential in such a hostile environment. Shirt pockets each had holes sewn into their bottoms so that water could drain out and trousers had side pockets sewn onto the thighs (also with drainage holes). Boots had special grooves cut into the soles to enable them to cope with slippery, red mud and there were holes in the arch of the boot to allow water to drain out. Of particular interest is the sheet of metal hidden within the moulded sole of each spike protective boot. This was another development introduced to counter the specific operational conditions soldiers encountered in Vietnam. Previous to the introduction of such protective measures, unwary American soldiers frequently stepped on sharpened bamboo stakes, or 'punji sticks' – lethal spikes smeared with faeces to ensure infection if they pierced the sole and concealed by enemy soldiers and Vietcong guerrillas to slow down any US advance. Today's US troops still use the same design of footwear.

North America's famous ERDL, or Experimental Research Development Laboratories, are responsible for some of the most elaborate and collectable US uniforms worn during the Vietnam War; the various camouflage patterns worn during the conflict. The most highly prized uniforms are the early 'duck hunter' and 'tiger stripe' uniforms worn by US military advisors, Special Forces troops and South Vietnamese rangers. Most of the original ones were made in Vietnam by the Vietnamese, but they are so popular they

A member of the Royal Observer Corps with an OC-marked British Mk II helmet, headset and chest microphone for telephone communication. It is early in the war because he's still in civilian clothes and only wears the OC brassard and enamel badge. Slung over his left shoulder is a military pattern respirator in haversack. Photographed at the Kent Battle of Britain Museum, which is located at Hawkinge, a frontline Fighter Command airfield in 1940, the observer stands in front of a hexagonal brick and concrete Airfield Defence pillbox.

This reconstruction shows a German infantry scout section reconnoitring routes suitable for tanks to pass through the 'impregnable' Ardennes forest during *Fall Gelb* (Case Yellow), the German armoured thrust towards the river Meuse and on into Northern France in May 1940. The soldiers wear the Model 1936 uniform trimmed with white *Waffenfarbe* (arms colour) to denote their arm of service (infantry). Featuring round rather than pointed ends, their tunic epaulettes are of the second pattern, introduced in 1938. Festooned with personal kit, which included their black *Koppel* (belt) strung with *Patronentasche* (cartridge pouches), a *Kochgeshirr* (cook pot), *Brotbeutel* (bread bag), *Tragbuschse für Gasmaske* (gas mask canister), *Feldflasche* and *Trinkbecker* (field flask and drinking cup), *kleine Shanzzeug* (small entrenching tool), as well as a bayonet and scabbard and gas case, not to mention weapons and ammunition, it's hardly surprising the enlisted man in the foreground looks tired. Also of interest is the design of the elasticated webbing straps, which could be hooked onto the helmet lip to retain pieces of foliage for added camouflage.

have been reproduced for many years. So make sure you know what you are buying and ask for written evidence of provenance if at all possible. Not as sought after or as expensive as Vietnam War period uniforms, modern US digital camouflage patterns, known as the Universal Camouflage Pattern, designed for use in woodland, desert, and urban environments, and seen on TV in action in current operational theatres in the Middle East and Afghanistan, are of consideration for the novice looking to build an interesting collection.

In December 2009, BBC News announced that 'the uniform of the British Army is to be changed for the first time in almost forty years.' The bulletin went on to explain that the British Army's new 'Multi-Terrain Pattern' (MTP) was to replace the traditional

This photograph illustrates both USAAF (United States Army Air Force – an independent US air force didn't exist until 1947) and RAF WWII uniforms. The American officer is wearing one-piece green Army Air Force flying overalls and an American aircrew pattern parachute harness. Also visible is a yellow 'Mae West' life preserver, which was invented in 1928 by Peter Markus and earned the famous nickname because wearers were thought to resemble the well-endowed Hollywood film star of the same name. This figure also wears an officer's pattern peaked service cap, often called a 'crusher'. The term was derived from 'fifty mission crush', a tradition started in the 8th Air Force to denote veteran flyers who removed the caps' stiffeners – a wire around the inside top perimeter to maintain a cap's round shape. However, there was also a practical purpose because pilots wore headsets over their caps during flights and removing the wire stiffeners made the headgear more comfortable.

four-colour woodland uniform, or 'No. 8 Disruptive Pattern Material'. Forces in Afghanistan were scheduled to be the first to get the new uniform with the entire army upgraded by 2011. One reason for the introduction of the multi-terrain MTP uniform was the need for operational duty in a wide range of environments inside Afghanistan, especially in Helmand Province with its mix of desert, agricultural 'green zone' either side of the Helmand River, and residential areas comprising dusty buildings and mud huts. Lieutenant Colonel Toby Evans, a military advisor with the Government's Defence Science and Technology Laboratory, told the BBC that the new uniform was a compromise between having a uniform that was perfectly suited to a specific environment and one that would work well across a wide range of conditions. He said:

'We've realized that Afghanistan is more complex – especially Helmand – than, say Iraq, which was predominantly a desert background, or North-West Europe, which was predominantly green … the new camouflage is optimized for all the Afghan background colour sets and in so doing we never reach a point – which we did with the old colours – where it is actually wrong. It may not be quite perfect, but it's good enough for everything.'

Before we leave the subject of military uniforms behind, we must look, albeit briefly, at those uniforms worn by women. Of course, women's services had their own badges but the most obvious difference made to accommodate women in National Service was naturally in the cut of their clothing. One of the most iconic uniforms worn by women in Britain during both world wars had nothing to do with military service at all but was organized by the Board of Agriculture in 1915. Known initially as the Land Army during the First World War, by the end of 1917 thousands of women were soon working as supplementary farm labourers. With six million men away fighting all around the globe Britain was struggling for labour. Although many traditional farmers were at first against such female assistance, after the Board of Trade despatched an army of agricultural organizers to speak with farm owners they, were soon encouraged to accept women's work on the farms.

Today we are more familiar with the uniform of green jersey and brown corduroy breeches worn by members of the organization during the Second World War. Remembering the sterling work done by women some twenty years earlier, in June 1939 the Government established the Women's Land Army. By 1944 the WLA had more then 80,000 members and lasted until its official disbandment on 21 October 1950. Together, the WLA and those farmers who were kept back from active military service because their vital job was considered a 'reserved occupation' transformed British agriculture during the Second World War. Indeed, Britain's 'war on the land' was just as vital as those more famous victories such as the Battle of Britain and El Alemain. By war's end Britain produced twice as much home-grown foodstuff as it did in the 1930s and every citizen was fed. Starvation, a real possibility once the U-boat campaign had reached its peak, didn't befall the British people.

Upon joining the WLA new recruits received two green jerseys and two pairs of breeches. They wore a distinctive hat or gumboots, an overcoat and an oilskin sou'wester in foul weather. Whatever the conditions, they wore the WLA's brassard on their left arm. This was green and featured a red crown and the letters 'WLA'. A series of half-diamond shaped badges were sewn on to identify their number of years' service. The WLA was the parent of another closely associated body, the WTC, or Women's Timber Corps. Only employed on forestry work, WTC members – colloquially known as 'Lumber Jills' – wore a similar outfit to their sisters in the WLA but topped it off with a green beret adorned with their own badge.

With the help of the Red Cross and the Order of St John, women's Voluntary Aid Detachments were first established in 1909. By the summer of 1914 there were more then 2,500 Voluntary Aid Detachments in Britain and many women eagerly offered their service to the war effort – two VADs went to France as early as October 1914. Soon the women's First Aid Nursing Yeomanry (FANY) and the Women's Army Auxiliary Corps were playing an important part in the war and on 16 January 1917, Lieutenant General H. Lawson recommended using women in the Army in France. By the spring of 1917, even Sir Douglas Haig, Commander-in-Chief of the British Army, had come round to the belief that women could play a part on active service, though not of course anywhere near the front line. The Women's Army Auxiliary Corps (WAAC) was the result. The WAAC uniform consisted of a small, tight-fitting khaki cap, khaki jacket and skirt. Regulations stated that the skirt had to be no more than 12 inches above the ground. The WAAC was organized into four units: cookery, mechanical, clerical and miscellaneous. The War Office stated that any job given to a member of the WAAC had to result in a man being released for front line duties. Women in the WAAC were divided into officials (officers), forewomen (sergeants), assistant forewomen (corporals) and workers (privates). Between January 1917 and the Armistice, more then 57,000 women served in the WAAC. After the WAAC was disbanded in 1921 women went back to their normal jobs, or at least were expected to, and the variety of duties they undertook just as well as men showed that, apart from combat duties perhaps, there was no reason to segregate the sexes as far as National Service was concerned. With this in mind, as storm clouds gathered during the late 1930s, the authorities decided to resurrect some of the organizations that had done so well during the First World War. As a consequence, on 9 September 1938 the Auxiliary Territorial Service – or ATS as it was more usually known – became the women's branch of the British Army during the Second World War. On 1 February 1949 it was merged into the Women's Royal Army Corps. In February 1945, a then eighteen-year-old Princess Elizabeth, our current monarch, joined the ATS as a subaltern and trained as a mechanic and truck driver. London's National Army Museum currently has the Queen's ATS brigadier uniform on show as part of a Jubilee exhibition. Featuring a wool barathea tunic made by London's Saville Row tailors Sandon & Co, it is adorned with the Queen's own medal ribbons, including the Royal Order of Victoria and Albert, King George V Silver Jubilee Medal 1935, the King George VI Coronation Medal 1937 and the British War Medal 1939–1945.

After the Second World War, it was recognized that women should have a continuous and more regular role to play in the armed forces and the 'women's services' were permanently established with WRACs (Women's Royal Army Corps), WRENs (Women's Royal Naval Service) and WAAFs (Women's Auxiliary Air Force) personnel joining their male colleagues on the parade ground.

The early 1990s saw the most dramatic peacetime changes in women's military duties in Britain and they rapidly became fully integrated on surface ships, as aircrew for the first time, and also assumed far greater responsibility in the Army. The previous segregation appeared antiquated and by the mid-1990s women's roles were fully assimilated into the three main service branches – the Royal Navy, Army and Royal Air

Force. The separate women's services were abolished. As early as 1942 unmarried women in Britain aged between nineteen and thirty were conscripted, with most being sent to the factories (if they hadn't volunteered for the ATS or other women's services) and by 1943 women were liable to some form of organized labour up to the age of fifty-one. Nazi Germany took far longer to enrol their womenfolk into some kind of war work. Women were not expected to work in Hitler's Germany and within months of the dictator coming to power, many female doctors and civil servants were actually sacked. Such was the skills shortage in Germany that in 1937 a law was passed that required women to do a 'duty year' to support the Reich. German girls were swept along in the spirit of Third Reich militarism, mainly as members of the Bund Deutscher Mädel (BDM, the League of German Girls – the girls' wing of the overall Nazi Party youth movement, the Hitler Youth). The Hitler Youth – or more properly, Hitler Jugend, abbreviated to 'HJ', was first formed in 1922 for boys between fourteen and eighteen (similarly the BDM catered for girls of the same age). Incidentally, young German boys and girls between the ages of ten and fourteen could join either the Deutsches Jungvolk or Deutsches Jungmädel respectively. Probably the other largest auxiliary wartime organizations employing women in Nazi Germany were the Luftwaffe, which employed a large number of female auxiliaries as Luftwaffe Helferinnen) and the RAD (Reich's labour service) which employed girls between the ages of fifteen and sixteen as Flakhelfer serving with the Flak. Finding any kind of original German women's uniforms from the Nazi period is a pretty forlorn quest, but occasionally things do turn up. It's easy to find surviving examples of uniform insignia though and I'm fortunate enough to have an example of a BDM arm band in my collection.

The United States established its own Women's Army Auxiliary Corps (WAAC) in May 1942. From September 1943 the Women's Army Corps (WAC) became an integral part of the Army of the United States. WAC officers and warrant officers had to buy their own military clothing but enlisted women continued to receive their uniforms free, as did enlisted men. By the end of 1944, the Army Nurse Corps had adopted the WAC service uniform of raincoat, overcoat and accessories.

The Second World War WAC winter-service uniform consisted of a wool, olive drab skirt, jacket, and a cap with visor, commonly called the 'hobby hat'. A belt originally issued with the uniform (summer and winter) was eliminated in late 1942 because it wore out the material beneath it. The summer-service uniform was identical in style to the winter uniform but was made of lighter cotton material and manufactured in a khaki shade. In June 1954 all US Second World War women's uniform items were declared obsolete. WACs stationed in Europe received a waist-length, olivedrab wool jacket called a 'battle jacket', which could be worn with matching skirt or slacks.

During the post-war era (1945–1950), women's uniforms changed little. In March 1946 women could buy and wear brown leather pumps of plain design and in 1946, nylon hose were issued for the first time to army women. But they had to be careful that the seam down the back of their leg was always straight! The last uniform change

This photograph shows the somewhat typically ramshackle appearance of a member of the Home Guard in the summer of 1940. A volunteer from a battalion affiliated with the Royal West Kent Regiment, he wears ill matched battle dress denims, a cloth bandolier full of spare magazines and a civilian gas mask in its box. The rifle he carries is another rough and ready expedient. Consignments of the US WWI vintage Springfield P17 arrived from America packed in thick grease, which had to be laboriously cleaned off before the weapon could be test fired. Furthermore, it was of .300 calibre, unlike the British Lee-Enfield SMLE, which fired a .303 calibre round. Consequently, to avoid confusion between the P17 and the SMLE, a 2-in-wide red band was painted on the US weapons and quite often '300' was also stencilled on the red band as well.

in the post-war era was the substitution of a dark olivedrab tie in 1949 that replaced the cotton khaki necktie – this change applied to both men's and women's uniforms.

'Dressed to Kill: US Army Finally Designs a Female Uniform that Fits,' shouted a headline in *The Independent* in April 2011. The reported added: 'The women of the US military will still be wearing trousers, but from now on they might actually fit. In a move that highlights the changing nature of traditional gender roles, the Pentagon is road-testing its first ever range of combat uniforms designed specifically for female recruits.' It went on to say that considering that roughly fourteen per cent of the members of America's armed forces are women, and that 220,000 have served in Afghanistan and Iraq the move to design uniforms which actually catered to their particular needs was, to say the least, timely. Former Army Staff Sergeant Maria Canales told the Associated Press that during her Iraq deployment in 2005 and 2006, her body armour was painfully snug. She later upgraded to a larger suit, but that made her worry about safety. She said: 'Thank God, nothing happened where my body was compromised … it was looser and I guess that's the disadvantage because if … we have contact, it would be easier for something to happen.'

Major Sequana Robinson, who is working on the trial of new kit at Fort Belvoir, was at pains to stress the new outfits would not unduly showcase female curves. She said: 'It is not, not a form-fitting uniform. It's just a uniform that's based on female body dimensions. It's less material because women are different than men.'

No account of women in military or auxiliary service during wartime can be at all complete without mention of those brave girls, some 800,000, who served in the Soviet armed forces in the Second World War. Unlike all the other belligerents who enrolled female recruits into purely auxiliary roles, a huge number of the USSR's women were employed in front-line duties. The most famous unit, I suppose, must be Aviation Group 122, which comprised three regiments: the 586th Fighter Aviation Regiment, the 46th Taman Guards Night Bomber Aviation Regiment and the 125th Guards Bomber Aviation Regiment. Together these regiments flew a combined total of more then 30,000 combat sorties and produced more than thirty 'Heroes of the Soviet Union', the USSR's highest award.

Not as glamorous as the many Soviet aviatrixes perhaps, Stalin's female snipers exacted a heavy toll on the motherland's enemy. Two of these were Nina Alexeyevna Lobkovskaya and Lyudmila Pavlichenko, who shared more then 300 confirmed kills between them. Born in 1925, Lobkovskaya even participated in the Battle for Berlin when only nineteen years of age.

The above is merely the sketchiest survey of women's roles in two of the world's major armed forces, at least. Women have been integrated into the military of most other nations for just as long. This book is not the place to look in detail at women's costumes but from the very few items on these pages, collectors will see that the area of female military uniform and insignia is as rich and varied as that of their male counterparts. In Britain, especially in the Second World War, there is enough variety of uniforms worn by women in the numerous auxiliary services to fill a book. Fortunately, for those who want to find out more about the type of Norfolk-cut jackets, navy slacks or khaki skirts worn by women in the myriad of organizations like the Air Raid Precautions (ARP) services, Auxiliary Fire Service (AFS) or the Women's Auxiliary Police Service (WAPC), there's a whole library to choose from.

Chapter 3

Military Equipment

O nce upon a time collectors of militaria contented themselves with badges and perhaps supplemented their accumulation of vintage bits and pieces with a tunic or helmet. Those with deeper pockets or who possessed the ability to repair engines or were perhaps wealthy and proficient at mechanics might be lucky enough to own a vintage military vehicle such as a US Jeep or British Morris utility vehicle. Today, the military equipment category is much wider and enthusiasts procure a bewildering array of hardware either used in the field by the military or which played a part in the civilian life of the Home Front. Not surprisingly, therefore, military equipment covers an enormous array of paraphernalia and is a pretty big category, covering everything from the personal gear soldiers carry into battle to the first aid kits carried by air raid wardens during the Blitz. This category also covers everything that doesn't neatly slot into more obvious sections like uniforms, regalia and headgear. In fact, it doesn't seem to belong anywhere, but individual collectors cherish it all with abandon!

The current vogue for military re-enactment and the dramatic increase in educational outreach programmes and living history groups has seen a big increase in current demand for authentic military field equipment. Civilian and paramilitary utility items are also popular accessories for use in displays involving vintage military vehicles or exhibitions of 'how we lived then' at schools and museums. Unlike uniforms and badges, which are relatively easy to reproduce or fake, chunky items like air-raid sirens, jerry cans, folding camp beds and Air Ministry bomb sights are very difficult to copy.

Since the World War Two Battle Re-enactment Association (WWII BRA) kick-started the organization of large-scale public events featuring vehicles and combat-dressed soldiery such as the legendary Battle of Molash in the 1970s, on to the massively successive War & Peace shows held annually at Beltring in Kent, there has been a huge upsurge in such outdoor activities. At last collectors have been able to banish the image that they spend their lives locked away inside cleaning and counting their hordes of knick-knacks. At outdoor events like the one at Beltring they emerge into broad uplands and sunshine, although it has to be admitted that they are often dressed head to foot as Wehrmacht infantrymen of US Vietnam 'grunts'!

Curiously, this recent upsurge in interest for full-size collectables, including classic military vehicles, has encouraged the fusion of previously disparate collecting interests. Today, collectors of more esoteric field equipment such as radios, who may have begun their hobby while a radio ham or valve radio enthusiast and then gradually become interested in vintage wireless sets, have discovered that military auto jumbles and re-enactment fairs are a source of collectables. Previously, they might have had little to do with military collectors but now embrace them as very useful contacts. All this 'cross-pollination' has encouraged greater interest in the wider area of Second World War battlefield communications and has spawned a wealth of useful material to add to the canon of literature about military history. Field radios, portable military telephone units, exchanges and even collectable cable drums are now the kind of objects that change hands at such fairs or, increasingly of course, online. Indeed, quite recently the respected French publisher Heimdal produced *Les Materiels Radio de La Wehrmacht* (German Radio Sets 1935–1945), so dealers can expect a run on 'Torn.Fu.d2' sets as this book fuels demand for them. Radios and field telephones might be pretty specialized and of only esoteric appeal but their popularity reveals the breadth of this category within the entire military equipment field. Some other things are perhaps of more of obvious appeal.

For a long time, items of webbing – the belts, pouches, packs and gaiters, which along with helmet and rifle completed battledress – were the most commonplace and inexpensive articles. Now, even they are in short supply. In fact it's an indication of just how much was produced during wartime and perhaps how long the war might have continued in the Far East if Japan hadn't succumbed to the atom bomb, that so much was produced. Nick Hall, proprietor of well-known dealership Sabre Sales, recalled that soon after the Second World War a huge quantity of British webbing was burnt to release the brass fittings – a valuable component and worth money if melted in quantity. Nick also remembered he'd been promised a huge amount of really quite rare maritime bicornes and ceremonial helmets, held in stock for aeons by military outfitters Gieves & Hawkes. When he arrived to take possession of these quite rare items, he was dumbfounded to discover they had been burnt to release the precious metals in the bullion used on the regalia decorating them. Collectors have Britain's Royal Navy to thank for the fact that despite so much recycling, a great deal of authentic webbing has survived. Apparently, the 'Senior Service' retained their huge stocks of '37 Pattern webbing until well into the 1990s. See, you never know when it might be needed. Despite this, enthusiasts should note that there is generally thought to be very little authentic British Second World War webbing in circulation. Much of it sold

WWI British soldier's D-Type two-piece mess tin, white cotton housewife sewing kit, home-made identity bracelet of sapper in the Royal Engineers, set of later issue ID discs belonging to an RFA gunner (the secondary round disc would have been attached to a box respirator or its haversack after its introduction in late 1916).

today as being worn in battle by a British regiment either originates from the former British Empire or is the product of skilful reproduction. So if you are after such items, now is the time to purchase them. Indeed, even good quality dated belts and bayonet frogs are now becoming hard to find and at one time these were ten-a-penny. Talking of British webbing, it has to be admitted that the Holy Grail of British '37 Pattern webbing has to be the pouch specifically designed to carry two magazines for the Browning High Powered Pistol – the automatic .45. When searching for one of these rare examples, collectors should look for the manufacturer's mark, often 'Z. L. & T. Ltd' and a date stamp on the inside of the holster's top flap.

Collectors of militaria, especially re-enactors, have long coveted original field dressing packs but many enthusiasts have now realized the hitherto overlooked potential of ARP

first aid kits. These, usually packed in haversacks like the well-known Paragon brand, come complete with a vast range of splints, tourniquets, ointments (often secured in delicate glass-stoppered bottles contained in silvered cylinders), knives and scissors. Complementing the survival-aid equipment carried by wardens and rescue squads are the numerous respirators available. Some, like the heavy-duty Civil Defence versions, came complete with microphones and earpieces to be worn by telephone operators during a gas attack.

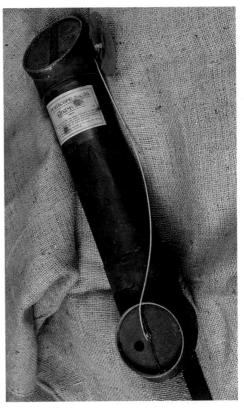

WWI British tubular trench periscope dated 1917, War Office issue. This was carried and used in a more mobile context than the larger boxed periscope permanently mounted on the fire step of a trench. However, it has removable aperture covers secured to the body with string. At its base is a moveable spigot for securing the periscope to the trench side.

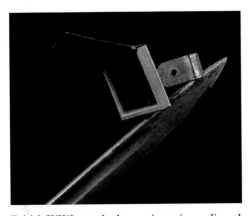

British WWI trench observation mirror clipped to the 17-in bayonet of a short magazine Lee-Enfield rifle and allowing oblique study of hostile terrain. The Army had thought about this as long ago as 1914–1918 – so much for Tom Hanks having to use chewing gum in *Saving Private Ryan*!

Children were encouraged to don simpler gas masks, of the type dubbed 'Mickey Mouse' by virtue of the separate 'goggle eyes' and snout-like filter casing. Mint examples of standard British Second World War civilian respirators, complete in their original cardboard boxes (threaded with a length of string or held inside commercially manufactured containers for wear) and with instructions printed inside the lid explaining how to pack, unpack and wear the respirator, are also worth keeping an eye out for. These previously commonplace items are now eagerly collected.

Perhaps the most poignant examples of personal respirators are those designed for use by babies. The British version – a relatively large and cumbersome object – encased the whole child, leaving only the legs dangling free. The infant could be clearly seen through a large visor, rather similar to a space helmet. Being too young to draw filtered air with its own lungs, the child's survival depended on the ability of the mother to continue to operate a concertina-shaped rubber pump that forced air into the sealed container. Heaven knows what would have happened if the parent was injured, or indeed how long she was expected to pump until the all-clear was sounded. Interestingly, surviving examples of German infant respirators from the Second World War can still be obtained. As one might expect from a nation with a proud tradition for practical engineering, the German solution was ingenious, if not a little impersonal. Once secured within its gas-tight container, the German infant was supplied with air by the simple expedient of the mother operating a foot pump so baby could be suspended from a suitable hook while the mother continued to read or sew.

British ARP 'gas rattles' have, like gas masks and even the most nondescript Civil Defence helmet, achieved much more desirability in recent years. Collectors should study any rattles passed off as those used by wardens very carefully. Commercially produced football rattles were available in their thousands pre-war and to be fair, many used by ARP professionals started life on the terraces, but official ARP-stamped rattles can be found and are naturally more valuable. Intended to signify a chemical attack, rattles were only one facet of the ARP warden's public address equipment. To signify the all clear when a raid had passed and the poison gas had dissipated, brass handbells were used. As with rattles, these were often commercially produced items as used by schoolmasters and town criers, but pressed into civil service. Naturally, bespoke examples officially stamped with ARP insignia can be found

British military pattern 'box' respirator from WWII carried on the Home Front by 'essential' civilian personnel such as policeman, who needed the highest level of protection. The haversack still bears traces of the words 'Remote Breathing Apparatus' because this model enabled rescue crews to implement a 'buddy' – a shared-breathing system, similar to that used in scuba diving.

but at a premium price. ARP rattles and handbells are perhaps two military collectables that could be put on general display and certainly fit well within a Cath Kidston-inspired interior or as well as 1940s' washboards, drainers and towel racks do, at least. Why, the heavy brass handbells also make particularly useful paperweights!

Perhaps one area where collecting equipment, rather than insignia or combat clothing, is of particular interest to collectors is the category of aircrew equipment. For British collectors of RAF equipment the most sought-after items include the classic Type B leather flying helmet of Battle of Britain vintage. This helmet is easily identifiable by the two zip-fastened leather blisters enclosing the earphones. Manufactured from brown chrome leather, the helmet comprised six vertical panels meeting at a single narrow central ridge panel running from front to rear. It had a rectangular horizontal panel across the forehead and the two previously mentioned zipped, padded-leather oval housings to the ears and leather chinstrap (secured by a metal friction type Bennett buckle). The adjustable leather strap ensured a snug fit and facilitated ease of removal of the helmet. Lined with buff-coloured chamois, the helmet's ear cups were padded for comfort. To compliment this helmet many collectors seek a pair of RAF Mk IV flying goggles with all the fittings, such as the removable sun shield (to enable the pilot to look out for the dreaded 'Hun in the sun'). These goggles featured distinctively large ear loops, which were created to fit over the substantial and prominent ear domes. Finding

one in its original box, complete with accessory screwdriver to facilitate altering the fittings, is little more than a dream, but those who dare win.

To complete the perfect early flying helmet combination a Type D oxygen mask/microphone attachment should be added – if you can find an original one. Fitted with an RAF Type 21 microphone and switch, the mask enabled pilots to communicate with each other – essential if they had spotted a marauding enemy aircraft. Interestingly, it was the successor to the famous Battle of Britain period masks the yes –you guessed it –Type E oxygen mask which was the first in RAF service to use the economizer flow system whereby oxygen was released from the supply only when the wearer actually inhaled. This system may have conserved precious oxygen but due to the fact that the inlet/outlet tube had a shared operation

Despite enemy action, some work had to go on as usual. GPO (General Post Office) telephonists still had to connect vital calls – even if there was a gas attack. Consequently, specialist gas masks were manufactured, like this one, enabling an operator to connect plugs with jacks in the plug board regardless of a chemical attack by the enemy.

(incoming cold dry oxygen meeting warm and moist exhaled breath, which would condense) it was prone to freezing and consequent blockages. Not helpful at all at 'Angels 15' (15,000ft)! Original type D masks are as rare as hens' teeth and most collectors are forced to opt for reproduction versions, but these aren't cheap, selling for as much as £500.

Original flying helmets and goggles are a bit easier to find but be ready to dig deep here too. At the time of writing (Oct 2012) I found an original RAF type B helmet on eBay for a tidy £600 and a couple of sets of MIV goggles, one for £500, the other, which came in its original box, for £750. It is still possible to find examples of somewhat less expensive RAF flying helmets and the classic type C helmet, introduced in 1941 and did sterling service for the RAF well into the 1950s, is probably the most common 'vintage' type available. Although also well made from leather, the rubber cups protruding from the earpieces, rather than distinctive leather zippered hemispheres as featured on the type B easily, identify it. These rubber embellishments were used to secure headphones. The rubber type G oxygen mask accompanied the type C. Pilots generally opted for the classic Mk VII, leather padded goggles of the type also worn by most 1950s' and early 1960s' motorcyclists. I recently saw an original pair of Mk VII goggles sell for £475. Fortunately there is a very healthy repro market for such goggles, which are coveted by collectors and vintage motorcyclists, especially those that come complete with flip down sun visor. Such copies can be purchased for well under £200.

Third Reich SA Sturmabteilungen (SA Stormtrooper, or Brownshirt) dagger presented to 'accepted' members of the SA. Even rarer than this desirable model are the versions bearing the signature of SA leader Ernst Rohm on the blade reverse. These signed versions were presentation pieces that would have been issued to a chosen few prior to Rohm's assassination in 1935.

Third Reich German Luftwaffe officer's dagger. From members of the military and party administrators in the railways, even forestry officials, the NAZI state instigated daggers for every conceivable organization. They were designed as a symbolic representation of a badge of office. Together with NAZI insignia and headdress, these items probably rank amongst the first WWII souvenirs collected, being much prized by Allied soldiers, who eagerly 'liberated' them from their owners. Being such highly prized battlefield souvenirs, they were heavily copied in a surprising range of quality finishes. Often, surviving daggers have missing or replaced pommels, hilts and handles – so the collector has to be vigilant. As always, value is dictated by condition, the highest prices being commanded by examples with their hangers and knot intact.

Original Second World War RAF 'Mae West' life preservers and complete parachute and harness assemblies can only really be found in museums. The originals were always returned to depot storage and the life preservers featured a lot of perishable, rubber components, which meant few complete examples survived anyway.

As with RAF gear, Luftwaffe flying helmets are probably the most sought-after pieces. The basic helmet came in two versions; a lightweight canvas one for use in summer (worn by many of the crews during the Battle of Britain, of course) and a heavier version made from leather and much similar to the RAF equivalent. The earphone fixtures on Luftwaffe helmets are very different and have the earphones secured in slim moulded enclosures. Luftwaffe microphones were also quite different. Unlike the RAF's solution, Luftwaffe microphones were remote from oxygen masks. Consisting instead of discreet throat microphone incorporated into the helmet's neck strap. Ideally, collectors of Luftwaffe flying equipment should possess a pair of the classic shatter-proof Nitsche & Gunther goggles. Prospective purchasers of these large one-piece goggles should carefully examine the rubber surrounds of the eyepieces as, because of their age, it is

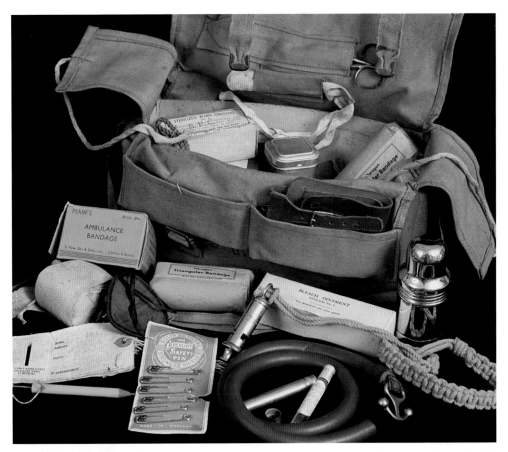

Contents of ARP first aid haversack, including various sized dressings, tourniquets, an eye patch, pills and ARP metropolitan whistle with yellow-braided lanyard.

This recognition model of a Mosquito fighter bomber is, like its subject, manufactured from a laminate material – paper, not ply, like the 'Wooden Wonder'. Very fragile, this miniature (made to the 1/72nd scale and pioneered by James Hay Stevens' 'Skybirds' models pre-war) still bears traces of its original decals.

very likely that the light coloured material is partially perished.

Whereas British and Allied life-preservers were inflated and could be punctured, early Luftwaffe versions were far simpler. Indeed, the classic Luftwaffe version worn by German aircrews during the Battle of Britain period consisted of sausage-like lengths of material filled with kapok. Again, these can only really be found at museums. Some of the finest examples in Britain can be found at the Kent Battle of Britain Museum at Hawkinge. In fact, there's a huge amount of very collectable Battle of Britain period flying equipment at Hawkinge, both RAF and Luftwaffe. This is quite fitting because as many readers will

'Paragon' commercially produced ARP first aid kit in rubberized cotton haversack. A good example of opportune marketing with contemporary first aid goods – bandages, splints, lint and medicine glass – packaged in a haversack marked ARP.

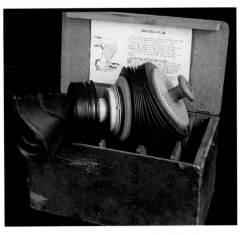

WWII British Home Front period hand-pumped oxygen resuscitator used by First Aid Parties in an attempt to pump air into the lungs of those overcome by smoke inhalation. 'Work the bellows steadily at about sixteen strokes a minute,' advised the instructions on the box lid.

In the 1930s it increasingly looked as if there would be another war and fear of aerial attack by poison gas was a major concern. This is hardly surprising when we consider how many people knew of family members who had succumbed to the effects of chemical warfare in the trenches during WWI. Consequently, ARP wardens were given specific equipment and training in the event of a gas attack. Wooden rattles were used to signify 'Gas!' and hand bells were rung for the 'All Clear!' Both of the examples shown here are marked ARP.

know, RAF Hawkinge was a front-line airfield during 1940. It was situated inland, high above the cliffs and a stone's throw from the area dubbed 'Hell's Corner'.

In the United Kingdom until around twenty years ago, other than service rifles that had been smooth-bored so they were classified as shotguns and kept on shotgun certificates, it wasn't possible to legally collect twentieth-century military firearms. Apart from a very few re-enactors who had applied for, and been granted, a Firearms Certificate, possession of the classic service rifles was beyond the scope of most collectors. It was only with the official acceptance of certificated deactivation that enthusiasts were able to own non-firing examples of everything from military handguns, rifles, automatic machinepistols, to heavy machineguns and even mortars. Coincidentally, around this time there were still large stocks of Second World War vintage weapons in the ordnance reserves and government stores – especially in Australia and other Commonwealth countries. As their arsenals were redeveloped, many of these developing economies earned considerable foreign exchange by selling obsolete weapons, many of which had been coated in grease and packed away since the First World War. As a result of these weapons being made available, the market was awash with British weapons and fortunately the trusty .303

Lee-Enfield, the mainstay of the British Army for more then half the twentieth century, became particularly common. Some of these recently deactivated weapons are models that were in fact obsolete by the Second World War, meaning such items as the .445 Webley pistol, Lee-Metford rifle and Lewis Gun commanded sky-high prices. Of these, the Lewis gun is perhaps the most rare and coveted. It is assumed that with the introduction of the Bren gun in the late 1930s, the majority of existing Lewis guns were scrapped but as every military enthusiast knows, this and the perhaps more famous Vickers machine gun play a key part in the unfolding story of British firearms in the twentieth century. Until the arrival of deactivated original weapons, collectors and re-enactors without firearms certificates had to make do with replica full-scale weapons of the kind that were imported from the Far East and enormously popular with enthusiasts in the 1970s. At this time, many a weapons mount on classic military vehicles carried an Asian

Some original WWII collectables can still be picked up for pocket money. Scour car boot sales and collectors' fairs for items such as this British Army 1937 pattern webbing water bottle cradle and standard issue felt-covered water bottle. At the time of writing these could be picked up for as little as £5.

facsimile of a real weapon, and very good many of them, were, too. Since the first wave of legislation restricting the ownership of certain deactivated weapons came into force in the 1990s (a natural reaction to the outrages perpetrated by crazed gunmen even in Britain) the laws of supply and demand have greatly affected the values of deactivated display weapons. The initial legislation principally affected semi-automatic rifles and sub-machineguns and prohibited the inclusion of moving parts in the breeches of such weapons that allowed them to be cocked. As a result, prices for the dwindling supply of such weapons sold and certificated before the introduction of the new rules has jumped. US M1 Garrand rifles and German MP40 sub-machineguns have more than trebled in value in less than a decade. Some weapons, like the famous British Martini-Henry rifle from the later part of the nineteenth century, are exempt; the authorities presumably think that few would attempt to hold up a bank with a weapon most people see on TV every Christmas when *Zulu!* is screened. Seriously, the reason these weapons have been spared is that being of an obsolete calibre, ammunition for operating versions of these weapons would be nigh on impossible to source. Furthermore, many modern bolt-action rifles such as the Lee-Metford and even the Lee-Enfield are now more then a hundred

Plane spotting was an essential routine both for the Royal Observer Corps (an observer's badge, headphones and chest microphone can be clearly seen) and the 'air-minded', socially responsible children and adults who scoured the skies for enemy aircraft. To support the huge demand for information that might help an observer tell friend from foe, a huge range of publications and spotters' guides were available during WWII.

years old and eligible for classification as antiques. For the first time, classifying a weapon as an antique or a firearm simply by definition of its age will no longer be relevant. Very soon many prohibited semi-automatic weapons and machine pistols, like for example the German Army's first sub-machinegun, the Bergmann MP 18.1, a 9mm weapon were introduced by the Central Powers in 1918. Even though this will very shortly fall into the classification of 'antique' it possesses a mechanism explicitly banned by the current firearms legislation. At the time of writing, collectors and especially re-enactors have been concerned about further changes in British law concerning the sale and ownership of antique firearms. This is understandable given the rise in firearms abuse, as previously possession of operating pistols, rifles and automatic weapons has long been restricted and, as we know, even modern deactivate, pistols or deactivated automatic weapons with partially working mechanisms are prohibited too. There's real concern that things might tighten up even further, preventing re-enactors from mustering in the fullest combat equipment. The latest published crime survey shows that government intervention has resulted in a reduction in violent crime by an impressive thirty-four per cent so it's hard to argue with a lot of the new measures but military enthusiasts owning muzzle-loading flint and wheel-locks or percussion-firing antiques, and especially those collectors of previously deactivated weapons, have been in a quandary about the legal status of their collections. During a debate on 26 March 2006, *Hansard*, the British Government record, quotes Baroness Scotland of Asthal, Home Office Minister of State, who recommended that the Violent Crime Reduction Bill be returned with amendments to the Commons for the second time, as saying: 'The definition (of the act) specifically excludes deactivated firearms and imitations of antiques, as well as any imitations that are antiques in their own right. I know that some collectors of real antique firearms are concerned that we have used 1870 as a reference point when there is no fixed date for antiques in the firearms acts. I should explain that this date was chosen because it was only after then that the manufacture of a particular type of breech-loading firearm became widespread. I am happy to put on the record that we see this date as having relevance only to the Violent Crime Reduction Bill; it has no effect on the provisions of the Firearms Act 1968, which deals with the status of real antique firearms.' It is assumed that re-enactors and collectors who have long had to abide by the provisions of the 1968 Act will experience little change to the pursuit of their hobby. On an official British police website (Devon & Cornwall Constabulary) the author found the following piece under the heading 'Buying Deactivated Weapons': 'It is important that care is taken when acquiring any firearm that is described as deactivated. You should ensure that you are shown the proof house mark and certificate issued in respect of any gun deactivated in the UK since 1989.' Nevertheless, it must be admitted that the prolonged uncertainties relating to the status of deactivated weapons has encouraged many enthusiasts to dispose of their collections and many dealers to cease trading in them. Because of the confusion regarding the legality of buying and selling such inoperable weapons their value has also dropped significantly.

One more recent feature that's part of the hobby of collecting vintage weapons involves firearms that will never be used offensively. This involves what enthusiasts consider a valid part of battlefield archaeology and sceptics reckon is digging for scrap – unearthing rusty relics from beneath the surface of fields and amidst the foundations of building developments. The trade in such excavated ordnance has also stimulated the interests of local authorities, both here and abroad, concerned that ,sooner or later, an amateur military historian will disturb a cache of live explosives and trigger a disaster. Despite the bureaucratic, health and wellbeing pitfalls, when professional historians like Richard Holmes or Brian Knight unearth the corroded firing mechanisms of weapons, they often reveal detail that adds to the historic record of military dispositions on the

It was vitally important that civilians kept clear of UXBs (unexploded bombs) and that the fire and rescue services knew where facilities such as fire hydrants and stirrup pumps were located. This assortment of cloth and enamel temporary signage was produced for the London Metropolitan Borough of Lewisham in South London.

Somme or at Isandlwana, for example. Amateur digging often disturbs buried bodies or reveals items that have no accurate means of dating or specification.

Collecting edged weapons remains unchanged and attracts its own enthusiastic collectors. Because of their durability, edged weapons survive longer than cloth or leather artefacts, enabling collectors to possess objects of far greater age than those owned by military uniform aficionados. Probably the most popular edged weapon for collectors is the bayonet. Many of the collectors and re-enactors who own 'de-acts' – non-firing rifles – also own bayonets related to the weapon. Probably the most popular is the standard issue 17-in bayonet designed to fit that staple of the British Army, the .303 Lee Enfield, of which a staggering seventeen million were produced!

The famous knife bayonet of First World War vintage gave soldiers embarking on a bayonet the charge with the redoubtable SMLE Mk III rifle – developed as long ago as 1903 – a remarkable 6ft reach. No wonder few opponents waited around when charged by a section of screaming Tommies. Collectors of such bayonets are also likely to possess the spike bayonet, or 'pig sticker', introduced in 1941 when the Mk III was deemed obsolete to be replaced by the improved Mk IV. They are also likely to own the No.9 Mk 1 bayonet, the more traditional 'knife-edged' weapon that replaced the short-lived spike after the Second World War.

The SA dagger illustrated in this book is very desirable, though ironically not highly valuable. Ernst Rohm's organization numbered nearly 1,000,000 men at its height and each was issued with a dagger. The early ones – before its originator was removed during the 'Night of the Long Knifes' – bore Rohm's signature. Although thousands were dumped in case invading Soviet soldiers got the wrong idea by association, those bearing his name realize the highest prices.

As always, scarcity influences price. The one previously ubiquitous weapon, which didn't survive the First World War in quantity, was the Lewis gun. Those that were traded on the collectors' market achieved record prices although recently a 100 pristine examples of this famous machinegun came to light when the Kingdom of Nepal decided to dispose of its arsenal. Interestingly, this arms depot had, since the end of the nineteenth century, when it was under British mandate, been the depository for numerous obsolete firearms.

Larger objects of military equipment, being cumbersome to store – if not simply beyond the price range of most individual – are of most interest to re-enactment groups looking to enhance their displays at public events. Now that much of the smaller, more accessible items of authentic wartime militaria, such as badges and uniforms, have been snapped up by enthusiasts, novice collectors are forced to be satisfied with 'honest' reproductions. About the only original items left are those larger pieces of field equipment that before the advent of re-enactment events, no one wanted. Today, items such as cargo trailers, mine detectors, anti-aircraft mountings, artillery sights and field cookers are as eagerly sought as RAF type B flying helmets and German *Stahlhelms* used to be.

The pages of British magazines *Classic Military Vehicle*, *The Armourer* and *Skirmish* – the most popular publications for military vehicle enthusiasts, collectors of militaria and re-enactors – testify to the increased interest in larger military collectables. The first magazine includes articles about past and forthcoming vehicle rallies and fascinating features on individual soft-skin and armoured vehicles. Whilst one might expect to find ads for surplus Jeeps, Land Rovers and even tanks, some of the other things advertised make more surprising reading. Finding a tracked Volvo Snowcat Arctic Warrior, 1937 vintage Wehrmacht pushbike, British cold-war MOBAT anti-tank gun and even a First World War vintage United truck with a working four-cylinder Wisconsin petrol engine – amongst many other similarly rarities – is proof of the demand for such items. Collectors on this scale need large gardens and even larger garages! Likewise, *The Armourer*, jam-packed with articles about military uniforms and regalia, devotes space to the collection of rather more cumbersome objects such as military water bottles, silver-plated Nazi teapots, British Army rum jars and even inert ordnance. The re-enactors who comprise the readership of *Skirmish*, obviously satisfied with a good deal of reproduction material, use this august publication as the market place for equipment like entrenching tools, folding wirecutters and small packs. It should be remembered that a great deal of re-enactment focuses on conflicts from the Dark Ages, the Medieval period, the English Civil War and numerous seventeenth, and eighteenth-century battles. So, there are lots of articles about broadswords, chain mail and tricorn hats as well!

With interest in the Home Front activities of warring nations seemingly ever on the increase, the collection of Civil Defence items and especially equipment used by Britain's Home Guard, or the Volkssturm, the Third Reich's equivalent, are more popular than ever.

Chapter 4

Headgear

I think there are three iconic items that to many people are the most distinguishable pieces of twentieth-century military dress. And each of them is an army helmet. They are: the German Second World War helmet, the *Stahlhelm*; the US M1 helmet, in service from the Second World War right up until well after the Vietnam War; and Britain's inimitable 1915 Brodie shrapnel helmet, which with very slight changes remained in service until 1944.

Not surprisingly, collecting such military headdress is a perennial favourite amongst enthusiasts. One aspect of its popularity is, I guess, the fact that being so robust, it doesn't require special treatment, unlike more delicate items of military uniform that can tear, fade, go mouldy or be devoured by moths! Because nineteenth-century headdress is so very rare, it is generally out of the reach of the average collector and most enthusiasts opt for twentieth-century caps and helmets.

Berets and field service (FS) caps (side caps) are also very popular collectables, especially as the colour of the beret usually shows what type of regiment the wearer is from. The most well known is the British Parachute Regiment's 'red beret', of course.

Example of a WWI British officer's soft trench cap. This example is badged to the West Yorkshire Regiment. It has a cap strap that has been split and braided – this popular non-conformist touch was also adopted by Other Ranks (ORs) during WWI. Such soft caps provided no protection against shrapnel and it wasn't long before they were replaced by steel helmets.

WWI British ORs soft trench cap badged to a gunner in the RFA. It was introduced in late 1916, replacing the now impractical stiff service cap that could not be easily stored or carried when the new steel helmet was worn. This example is made of woollen cloth, although there are other versions made of a more drill type of cloth.

The range of British types available is surprisingly comprehensive. For example, khaki berets are worn by British Foot Guards, the Honourable Artillery Company and infantry regiments such as the Princess of Wales Royal Regiment (formally the Queen's, an amalgamation of many proud regiments including the Buffs, Middlesex Regiment, Royal Sussex and West Kents), the Royal Anglican Regiment and the Green Howards. On the other hand, light grey berets are the choice of the Royal Scots dragoon Guards, brown – the King's Royal Hussars, and black – the Royal Tank Regiment. Rifle regiments wear dark green berets and include the Devonshire and Dorset Light Infantry, Royal Gloucestershires, the Berks and Wilts Light Infantry, the Royal Green Jackets and the famous Royal Ghurkha Rifles. The choice available in British military berets doesn't stop with this large selection available. There are berets from more exotic regiments to collect, such as the Parachute Regiment's maroon example and the Special Air Service's beige versions to collect. The Intelligence Corps wear a cypress green beret and the Royal Military Police don a scarlet version. Most other British Army units wear navy blue berets, as do members of the Royal Marines and non-commando qualified Royal Marines (upon graduation, marines wear commando green-coloured headgear). The Royal Air Force and the RAF regiment naturally wear RAF blue-coloured berets. In fact, members of the Royal Tank Regiment, Army Air Corps, Parachute Regiment and SAS only wear their berets and shun the peaked Cap No. 1 Dress that appeared after the First World War when the old scarlet jacket gave way to dark blue. The Cap No. 1 Dress is almost universally disliked by serving soldiers – hence its nickname 'craphat'. The No. 1 dress cap features a

British WWI military helmet with covered edge (effectively 2nd production model), commonly referred to in collecting circles as a 'Brodie', being named after its inventor, John L. Brodie, who patented the design in 1915. Intended to be proof against 'shrapnel and falling objects', being pressed from a single sheet of steel, the new helmet was cheap and easy to produce.

Interior of British WWI Brodie helmet. Although it was improved, to all intents and purposes the head protection granted by helmets worn by British soldiers a generation later wasn't significantly better.

coloured cap band (red for all Royal regiments/corps), on which the regimental or corps badge is worn, a crown that may have coloured piping or a regimental/corps colour and a patent leather peak and chinstrap. Apart from the front of the cap receiving a stiffener in 1975 to make the cap above the peak almost vertical, it has remained virtually unchanged for nearly a century.

One of the favourite collectables is the battlefield helmet. These are naturally robust and unlike field service caps unlikely to be attacked by parasites like the dreaded moth (although I did have a particularly fine British Royal Engineers 'Arnhem' period paratrooper helmet in my collection and its leather sweat band was nibbled by mice!). Battlefield helmets are also pretty common. Durable as soon as a generally acceptable design has been found – and we are really talking about classic US or Soviet patterns – the shells can be recycled and used by the myriad armies of developing countries. Indeed, Egyptian troops sported Russian Second World War helmets at the time of the Six Day War and during the Indian-Pakistan conflict following independence and separation. Both belligerents wore British pattern Second World War shrapnel helmets.

French M1926 pattern 'Adrian' steel helmet. This was an improvement on the classic WWI design, being a more robust one-piece steel stamping. Interestingly, the famous French helmet was a first. Named after its inventor, General Adrian, a French officer fascinated to discover that one of his soldiers survived a rifle shot to the head because the 'Poilu' wore his mess tin beneath his cloth kepi. Soon after, many other countries realized the protective value of steel helmets. Also shown is a French model 1931 military respirator, complete with haversack. In line with British and US fashion, French respirators featured a separate filter, attached to the mask by a length of hose and carried in the haversack, which is in turn slung over the head and secured around the body for added security. Two pockets inside the haversack contain metal tubes of decontamination ointment, to be used only upon the commencement of chemical hostilities.

Overall, the most popular and copied design has to be the US Second World War MI helmet. These can still be found relatively easily, but as with all helmets, value resides in the quality and preservation of surviving helmet liners. This redefined shape was introduced in 1941 (replacing the First World War British-type design) and addresses its predecessors key deficiently – the lack of protection to the rear of the head and neck area. When used on campaign in Europe this helmet would be seen with a British-made net and chinstrap fastened across the rear.

Fabricating a US Airborne helmet (MI-C) requires only subtle modifications to the generic MI army helmet and can therefore easily be faked. Often these were converted innocently for use by re-enactors but with the passing of time have entered circulation as supposedly authentic

'82ndAirborne helmets as worn at Arnhem'!

The US Army tank crew helmet, once common, is now also harder to find. One of the reasons of course is the huge increase in 1:1 re-enactment with enthusiasts donning 'tankers' helmets when crewing a Second World War American armoured fighting vehicle (AFV). Authentic examples are of lightweight composition and are heavily padded, being essentially crash helmets. Recognizing the often hot, unventilated conditions their crews would be expected to fight within, American designers pierced the helmet shell with numerous ventilation holes. When this helmet, first appeared, crews were expected to wear a fabric inner helmet which featured a skirt to protect their necks but they found this

British WWII vintage side caps: a Glengarry of the Seaforth Highlanders, worn by both UK- and Commonwealth-associated Scottish units – this pattern being most typical with its red, white and green dicing; officer's FS army cap in quality barathea cloth – a privately purchased item with both bronzed regimental insignia (Royal Artillery) and buttons and an RAF ordinary airman's FS cap and brass badge, introduced just prior to WWII and replacing the previous stiff service cap with patent leather peak.

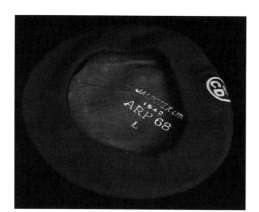

WWII British Civil Defence beret with cloth badge. A 'Basque' or 'schoolgirl' style beret, of larger diameter and without the leather trimming of standard military versions. It was worn in conjunction with the CD battledress, but because it is an ARP item it probably pre-dates the introduction of the complete uniform for CD services. The interior of the beret shows manufacturer, date, ARP stock number and size. Clearly marked and dated items command the highest prices.

Khaki tam-o'-shanter, or Balmoral, bonnet. Introduced in 1915 and worn by Scottish troops during and after both world wars, the example shown belongs to a Canadian Scottish unit, the Toronto Scottish. It is of Canadian manufacture. The badge backing is Athol grey (the kilt of the London Scottish – the UK regiment affiliated to the Toronto Scottish). All Commonwealth Scottish units were allied to a parent Scottish regiment.

WWII Fire Guard (FG) helmet. Although we are more familiar with wardens and rescue crews wearing the standard pattern Mk II steel helmet, like that in use with the armed forces, this version, known as the *Zuckerman* helmet, first appeared the middle of 1940. The dished design provided protection from falling masonry and offered more coverage for the head and neck area. It is also distinctive because the leather liner was attached to the helmet via the use of 'sewn-in' brackets.

German WWII Luftwaffe *Luftschutz* (air raid precautions service) helmet. A two-piece design different from armed forces helmets and of lesser quality. Across the front of the helmet is a transfer of the insignia of the *Luftschutz*. The helmet is constructed in sections for economy. German fire service helmets inspired its design. Lighter gauge steel than that employed in the construction of helmets for military service was another thrifty measure.

uncomfortable and most crews wore under it either the US Army knitted cap (the equivalent of the British soldier's cap comforter) or another favourite of US troops, the woollen Jeep, or Beanie cap.

In terms of design, the German Army's *Stahlhelm* has had the most influence. Protecting the lower neck – unlike the Tommy's battle-bowler, which was really only proof against falling shrapnel or debris – the 'Fritz' pattern helmet shape now equips the troops of most modern armies. Most collectors of militaria aspire to owning an authentic Second World War German helmet, preferably in its original finish, like the example from Roy Smith's collection shown in this book. With examples of the German Model 1916 version, especially the type converted to accept an additional 8mm armoured plate on the front to protect snipers, being beyond the reach of most, collectors are forced to seek out its successor, the similarly shaped 1935 model. As might be imagined, these come in quite a wide variety of finishes and those with evidence of original decals achieve

Classic British Army khaki WWII Mk II steel helmet. These went into production in 1938 to replace the WWI design. They resemble, but are a completely different stamping, from the previous model. The liner has been revised and improved as well. Though at the time many WWI shells were refitted with new liners and strap mounts to be designated MK1*. Each liner could be more easily changed as they were screwed and not riveted to the shell, which was a necessary feature because liners were made in the complete range of hat sizes. Note the earlier spring-sided web chinstrap, which would prevent injury should the helmet be lifted by blast.

German WWII M42 *Stahlhelm*. This version does not have the refined edge finishing of its predecessor (i.e. it has a non-rolled rim). The paint finish is referred to in collecting circles as 'Normandy' camouflage and follows that used on German military vehicles during late war (sand background oversprayed with lines of green and brown).

premium prices. Some German 1935 model helmets featured unusual turned-up brims and a very few issued to field signals troops and artillerymen featured cut-outs to enable the easy use of field telephones.

One of the most sought-after German Second World War steel helmets is the type issued to paratroops (Fallschirmjagers). Although under the pioneering leadership of Kurt Student, Hitler possessed airborne troops as early as 1936 it wasn't until 1938 that these Luftwaffe soldiers possessed their own helmet. Its style was quickly copied by the British (as indeed was the entire Nazis' concept of parachute forces, something that the Soviet Union had pioneered but had largely been ignored by the British until Hitler used airborne forces to such deadly effect during his invasion of France and the Low Countries in 1940). Finding these helmets is hard enough. Finding one complete with a camouflaged cover as introduced in 1941, is even harder.

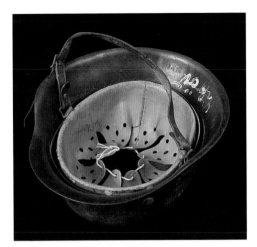

Interior of German WWII armed forces helmet showing leather cradle and chinstrap. Shells and liners of this type of helmet were block sizes so they would fit small, medium, large and extra-large head sizes. At the rear, painted in white, are the soldier's name and number, a common practice. Visible too, stamped in the metal, is the manufacturer's coded identity mark. This helmet doesn't bear any decals; after 1941, the German Army applied only one anyway. The single emblem denoted branch of service, the Army having done away with a decal of the national colours that was a ludicrous target (black, white and red – with a white stripe neatly in line with the occupant's temporal lobe!). This helmet is in excellent condition – original finish with chinstrap and liner intact. As ever, originality is the key to value.

WWII RN officer's pith helmet, accompanied by its japanned carrying box. In white finish to match the Navy's tropical 'whites', this helmet is identifiably of RN and not Colonial or RM origin by virtue of the blue band at the top of the folding 'Pugrie' headband. Similar helmets were worn by all three of the British armed forces. However, by WWII they were effectively obsolete. This is evidenced by the fact that, although part of the regular issue for troops in sunnier climes, they were frequently dumped on arrival in favour of the more practical bush hats, or steel helmets, once in theatre.

In keeping with the current trend towards the collection of items relating to the home front, both in Britain and abroad, there is increasing interest in Civil Defence helmets. Once, wardens' helmets and those worn by British rescue crews or firstaid parties were largely ignored. Often they were over-painted in khaki by re-enactors to accompany recreations of Second World War battledress. Today, even the most humble, rust-pitted Civil Defence helmet has value. Naturally, those with evidence of surviving stencilling achieve a higher price. One of the most desirable examples a of British Civil Defence helmet is the type fitted with an oiled canvas neck protector. Neck protectors were fitted to the helmets of rescue crews and wardens as a defence against the corrosive

Very rare Nazi WWII Allgemeine SS (Schutzstaffel) peaked cap. The more sinister of the Schutzstaffel branches (the other being the Waffen, or armed SS), the black-clad members of the Allgemeine spread terror wherever they served.

RAF leather type C flying helmet, without earpieces or wiring loom. Shown with a pair of Mk 8 flying goggles and H type oxygen mask without hose. The type C helmet came into use in 1942, but the H type mask was manufactured from late 1944 and wasn't WWII issue. Consequently, the arrangement shown is more typical of the late 1940s/Korean War period.

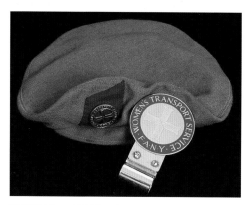

WWII First Aid Nursing Yeomanry/Motor Transport Corps women's barathea beret with cap badge. The organization was created in 1907 as a first aid link between front-line fighting units and field hospitals. The cap originates from the beret/bonnets worn by the organization's motor ambulance drivers during WWI. It has a value to collectors because the FANY was not supported by the War Office and was a rather quasi-private organization under the WO's umbrella. FANY essentially comprised women from 'the right background' and who held driving licenses. The badge is a standard bronzed FANY/MTC emblem, with burgundy lozenge backing. A very rare chromed vehicle mascot is also included in the photograph.

actions of chemical agents such as mustard gas – the *zeitgeist* of the time being the assumption of such attacks from the air. Collectors should examine surviving examples of helmets fitted with such neck shields with care, certainly before parting with hard-earned cash. As a result of being folded and stored for more then half a century, these protectors are often sticky and difficult to unravel. Furthermore, their oily composition often causes the rubber elements of chin straps and liners to perish.

As with all things, availability dictates value. Before the fall of the Berlin Wall in 1989, East German VoPo (Volkspolize*i*) helmets, as worn by some Army units and the Vopo Border Guard units, were

WWII US MI infantry helmet. Designed in 1941 as a replacement for the British Commonwealth issue helmet, the MI was conceived to offer better protection for the neck and lower head. In WWII some 70,000 US troops were saved by wearing the MI steel helmet – this is especially impressive considering the total killed was 368,000. In early versions of the helmet, the liner attachments, or 'bales', are fixed directly to the helmet shell; on later versions, including those worn after D-Day, the attachments swivel. Also, earlier liners are of a chunkier composition. The key thing about the earlier, more collectable, liners is that the internal straps (of either tan or green colour) are drawn together by a draw cord at the crown of the liner (rather than inter-lacing) and they feature a detachable nape strap at the rear of the helmet.

Interior of WWII US MI infantry helmet showing the webbing head cradle, which is part of the detachable liner (effectively a fibre helmet over which the steel shell fitted). A key feature of a WWII vintage GI helmet is tan strapping and the way these straps are drawn by a cord at the crown. There is a small rear nape strap and tan chinstrap. The leather liner strap passes over the front of the shell. Earlier MI helmet shells are identifiable by the non-flexible mounts that hold the chinstrap to the shell, and the join in the separate rim is at the front. Many of the features were faithfully copied by the Belgian and Dutch armies, who manufactured their own version after WWII. A collector must always bear this in mind when looking for an example of this helmet.

US armed forces Vietnam era steel helmet of 1960s' vintage. It was a remodelled version of the classic MI – the basic shape and the liner harness assembly being modified. The helmet shown features a reversible (summer/autumn) 'frog leaf' camo cover, with holes for mounting brush and an elastic retaining band into which myriad items, including insect repellent, gun oil and even toothbrushes, could be fitted. As was usual during this conflict, conscripted GIs often customized the finish of individual helmets to express their individuality.

Early-war black AFS (Auxiliary Fire Service) Mk II helmet.

British Mk II NFS green helmet with transfer, area number (14) in the rim.

National Fire Service WWII period women cap, post-1942 and the introduction of uniforms for the various civil defence organizations. The Civil Defence women's tunic and skirt were also adopted by female members of the NFS. This visor cap with earflaps, fitted with the NFS badge, was produced to complement the new outfit.

ARP controller's helmet. Rank markings using stripes (like these two for a senior rank) were adopted across Britain from 1942.

Green National Fire Service helmet with burgundy rank stripes and accompanying lettering, 'CFO' identifying a chief fire officer.

WWII British Civil Defence Mk II helmet worn by a senior First Aid Party member, identifiable by its colour, white, the letters, 'FAP' and the two black stripes.

Black-finish factory firewatcher's helmet. It features the hand-painted badge of the Morris Motor Company's fire brigade.

Mk II WWII British Civil Defence rescue party official. The white band denotes a team or section leader with the squad.

British WWII police helmet. The more common examples typically have the word 'POLICE' across their front, whereas this example has only the letter 'P'.

Mk II WWII British Civil Defence rescue party leader, finished in white.

Royal blue Civil Defence rescue party helmet No 2 Squad. Mk II WWII vintage helmets like this were extensively used by the civil defence corp. when it reformed in the early 1950s. It's possible this example could date from the later period.

With so many people killed and injured during the Blitz it was essential that clergy, often required to administer the last rites, wore protective clothing such as this very rare ecclesiastical ARP helmet.

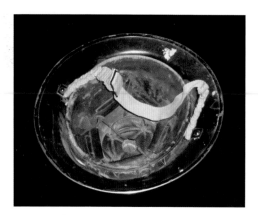

Interior of a typical British WWII Mk II ARP/CD steel helmet. Manufactured from manganese steel, each helmet weighed about 1.1kg. The chinstrap was made with cloth-covered springs and webbing. The springs were designed to expand should the brim of the helmet be caught by the upward force of a bomb or grenade blast, thereby reducing the risk of the wearer being throttled! Study the layout of the line – especially details of the cruciform rubber top pad and the rubber band surrounding the interior circumference.

Organizations like motor vehicle and arms manufacturers were large and important enough to the war effort to require their own internal ARP organizations. This Zuckerman pattern helmet belongs to the McEwan's brewery in Edinburgh. By the time of WWII, McEwan's, already famous for their Export India Pale Ale, were regularly supplying both the Royal Navy and the Navy, Army and Air Force Institutes (NAAFI) with kegged ales.

fetching a premium price on the militaria market. Now, despite many of these classic Soviet designs featuring fishnet camouflage netting and liner systems with chinstraps marked 'Made in East Germany', they are worth far less. When something is largely unobtainable, it's got value.

Chapter 5

The Home Front

The term 'Home Front' is most often associated with the Second World War, although it mustn't be forgotten that the first time British civilians, for example, were caught up in total war was some time before this, during the First World War. The citizens of Yarmouth were on the wrong end of German naval gunfire as early as November 1914, and a month later, in an effort to draw the Royal Navy into battle, the Kaiser's fleet shelled Hartlepool, Whitby and Scarborough. Dover wins the dubious honour of being the recipient of the first bomb dropped on British soil from a German aircraft when, on Christmas Eve 1914, Lieutenant von Prondzynski, his aircraft's joystick held between his knees, heaved a bomb over the side of his cockpit and dropped it towards the great naval harbour some 5,000ft below him. By the end of the war, a combination of Zeppelin airships and Gotha bombers mounted more then fifty air raids, dropped nearly 6,000 bombs and killed 557 people. Another 1,358 more civilians were injured and many families were left homeless.

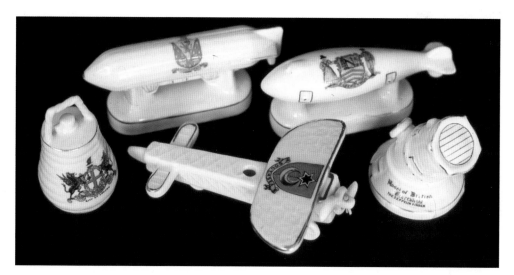

A selection of WWI vintage crested ware souvenirs. These cheap china novelties were originally designed as seaside souvenirs but the coming of war, and specifically the threat of aerial bombardment, brought a whole new significance to a familiar ornament. The basket-like object on the far left is an aerial bomb, of the type dropped by enemy airships. A searchlight can be seen on the far right.

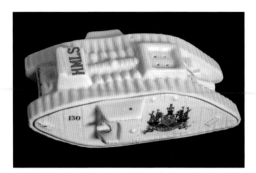

Carlton crested ware model of a WWI HMLS (His Majesty's Land Ship) bearing the coat of arms of the city of Southampton. In fact, this is a popular replica of *Crème de Menthe*, the tank commanded by Major Inglis DSO during the Battle of Flers-Courcelette in 1916, the first tank attack of the war.

'May God bless you until I return!' Mostly known today as 'silks', delightful embroidered postcards such as this were hugely popular during WWI. Many convents in Belgium and Northern France participated in the war effort as their nuns organized refugee workers to embroider simple and affordable postcards, which soldiers on active service could purchase to send home to their loved ones. Such was the demand from troops in the field that eventually Paris workshops employing assembly-line style workers to mass produce these souvenirs were established.

The First World War wasn't only the first time civilian populations were considered to be legitimate targets. It was also significant because it saw the mobilization of non-combatants, especially women. Between 1914 and 1918, it has been estimated that two million women were required to replace men in a wide range of jobs, many of them highly skilled in factories. More than worked as farm labourers in the Women's Land Army and 80,000 women served in the forces in a non-combatant role. New uniforms and special regalia sprang up with abandon, be they worn by female police officers, postal workers or bus conductors, and civilians working in factories making uniforms, guns, ammunition, tanks or ships were every bit as involved as the men at the front. Following the German submarine blockade of 1917, food rationing was introduced in January 1918, and previously uninvolved housewives felt they were doing their bit too. Not surprisingly given that it is now a hundred years since the First World War, very few authentic items relating to life on the Home Front survive. The conflict presented a seismic shock to the psyches of nearly all those alive at the time; virtually everyone had lost a friend, relative or acquaintance, and as soon as peace came in 1918 most right-minded people wanted to forget it. It's hardly surprising that the 1920s heralded a period of gaiety and women embraced the new liberties their recent emancipation promised. The carefree 'flapper' was born. Nevertheless, the enthusiast mustn't entirely discount the First World War period because there are one or two types of collectables dating from this period that are surprisingly easy to find.

'Zeppelin Brought Down in Flames' WWI postcard. William Leefe Robinson was the first British pilot to shoot down a German airship over Britain during WWI and he was awarded the Victoria Cross for his efforts. As this postcard testifies it was received as very good news by the British, especially coming so soon after the carnage of the Somme. We now know that the pilot destroyed a wooden-framed *Schütte-Lanz* airship, not Zeppelin L21 as was claimed at the time. In 1917 Leefe Robinson was shot down and captured by the Germans. He made several attempts to escape and was kept in solitary confinement as a punishment. His health failed and shortly after his return to England in 1918, he succumbed to the global flu epidemic, dying on 31 December that year.

Captain (Charles) Bruce Bairnsfather (1887–1959) is the famous creator of the iconic character of Old Bill and the illustrator of numerous famous cartoons such as those published in *Fragments from France* (1914) and *Bullets & Billets* (1916). That 16-inch Sensation is from the last of six sets of *Fragments from France* postcards published by *The Bystander* (there are fifty-four cards to collect). The illustration is self-explanatory and crystallizes the enduring fear of all infantrymen subjected to shelling ('whizz-bangs'). Bairnsfather understood their experiences, having joined the Royal Warwickshire Regiment in 1914 and immediately serving in the trenches of the Western Front.

Perhaps the most common items that can still be collected with relative ease are cigarette cards and period postcards. Beginning life in 1879, the year in which several American tobacco manufacturers began putting small card stiffeners into the flimsy paper packs of cigarettes to protect the contents from damage, cigarette cards remained in favour until the 1940s. From simple packet stiffeners the cards soon evolved into sophisticated illustrated customer loyalty premiums. For many people collecting the various series of illustrated cards, usually numbering fifty or so, in a set and then pasting them into similarly themed decorative albums, was both enjoyable and informative. The huge variety in British regiments in the front line of the First World War, and new military inventions such as the tank and aeroplane, provided ready subject matter for British cigarette manufacturers. British companies like W.D. & H.O. Wills, Carreras and John Player & Sons invested a lot of energy in creating sets of striking cards that covered every conceivable topic. In 1917 a shortage of materials stopped the production of cards and they did not reappear until 1922, so any examples from the early war period are especially collectable.

With so many men away on active service during the First World War, postcards were an essential way for families to stay in touch with their loved ones. They are one area of ephemera that captures the social history of the First World War and brilliantly they express the mood of innocent patriotism that characterises the early period of the conflict. Used to reinforce morale, as a recruiting medium and to belittle the exploits of the enemy, postcards were addressed and dispatched by the million. Delicate silk-embroidered cards, sewn by French and Belgian civilians, were sold individually to soldiers, and posted in envelopes. Tommies sent them home to their families with abandon. Because they were protected by envelopes, these fragile missives often survive in very good condition. Sentimental verses and bawdy lampoons masked the fears of men enduring the mud of the Western Front, or

Podmore China (Hanley, Stoke-on-Trent, Staffordshire) crested ware commemorative statue of Nurse Edith Cavell. She was executed by the Germans in 1915 on charges of treason after it was discovered she was sheltering Allied soldiers in occupied Belgium. News of Cavell's treatment caused international outrage and the British Government even commissioned a Report of the Committee on Alleged German Outrages committed during the Invasion of Belgium in 1914. Cavell was perhaps not so innocent, having been recruited by Britain's Secret Intelligence Service (SIS). Furthermore, many of the other alleged German atrocities mentioned in the (Bryce) report turned out to be fictitious.

Crested ware model of the Cenotaph (unmarked), bearing the arms of the city of London.

the heat, sand and flies of Palestine. Perhaps the cards of Captain (Charles) Bruce Bairnsfather, which featured his best-known cartoon character 'Old Bill' and Bill's pals 'Bert and Alf', are the most iconic printed items from this period. Together with his numerous postcards, Bairnsfather's weekly 'Fragments from France' cartoons were published in *The Bystander* magazine throughout the war.

At the time of writing the BBC reported the discovery of a previously unknown postcard sent by Adolf Hitler when he was a soldier in the First World War. Featuring an image of a medieval castle in Nuremberg, the postcard was discovered while material was being collated for the 'Europeana 1914–1918 Project', marking the centenary of the outbreak the First World War. Posted by Hitler in 1916 when he was recovering from a war wound, the postcard was found in Munich, Germany. It has since been verified as authentic by Oxford University. Hitler sent the card to one Karl Lanzhammer, a dispatch runner in the same regiment, when the 27-year-old Hitler was recuperating from injuries away from the front. It read: 'Dear Lanzhammer. I am now in Munich at the Ersatz Battalion. Currently I am under dental treatment. By the way, I will report voluntarily for the field immediately. Kind regards, A. Hitler.' The original recipient of the postcard died in March 1918 but the card ended up in the hands of a collector whose son brought it to a family history road show event in Munich as part of the Europeana project. As all professional historians and amateur enthusiasts know, original examples bearing Hitler's handwriting are exceptionally rare and this apparently quite nondescript example of First World War ephemera is a significant addition to the archive of the period.

Crested ware and small china models of aircraft, tanks and myriad other items of military hardware present another pretty easy to source theme for collectors. Like postcards, they are poignantly sentimental relics of the First World War. Introduced following the advent of the railways, crested souvenirs were all the rage in the late nineteenth and early twentieth centuries. Trains enabled ordinary people to travel outside

Dead Man's Penny. Nearly a million men from Britain and its empire were killed during WWI. It was felt that the simple War Office telegram sent to the next of kin of the bereaved was insufficient and in 1917 the Government announced a competition to design a suitable plaque, offering a prize of £250 for the winning design. Mr E. Carter Preston of Liverpool was the eventual winner. The winning design comprised a 12cm disc cast in bronze gunmetal, which incorporated an image of Britannia and a lion, two dolphins representing Britain's sea power and the emblem of Imperial Germany's Eagle being torn to pieces by another lion. Beneath this was a rectangular tablet where the deceased individual's name was cast into the plaque. The plaque shown here commemorates the sacrifice of Gunner Edward Holland of the Royal Field Artillery (RFA). No rank was given as it was intended to show equality in their sacrifice. On the outer edge of the disc arethe words, 'He died for freedom and honour'.

A scroll, 27cm x 17cm, made of parchment and headed by the Royal Coat of Arms, accompanied the plaque. On it was written: 'He whom this scroll commemorates was numbered among those who, at the call of King and Country, left all that was dear to them, endured hardness, faced danger, and finally passed out of sight of men by the path of duty and self-sacrifice, giving up their own lives that others may live in freedom. Let those who come after see to it that his name be not forgotten.' Production of the plaques and scrolls began in 1919, with approximately 1,150,000 being issued. They are not uncommon but it is very difficult to find one not only complete with its original certificate but also with the original stout cardboard packaging intact.

the environs of their local town or village. For the first time city factory workers could travel to the seaside, escaping the heat and grime of their daily labours. This new found freedom encouraged the new tourists to bring something back home to prove that they had experienced something so different. Before long every seaside resort offered a range of souvenir china mementos, each bearing the crest of the local authority, be it Blackpool,

Reconstruction of a typical British air raid warden's post during WWII. Note the masked windows designed to prevent shards of glass flying free should individual panes shatter. Also shown are a poster instructing the occupant on the identification of enemy aircraft; a range of official and commercially; produced publications; a 'blackout lamp' (on the windowsill – note the baffle preventing its beam from being seen from above); a gas alarm rattle and gas all–clear handbell, and a fully equipped warden's first aid haversack. All these items are now highly collectable.

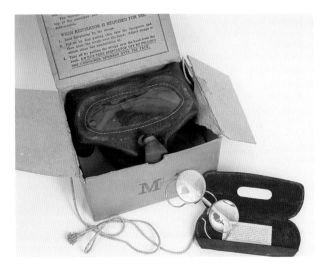

WWII British civilian respirator in its cardboard box, revealing care instructions on the reverse of the lid. The letter 'M' on the front of the box indicates that it's a medium-sized mask. This particular mask is a slightly different and more unusual version, having a black surround/seal to the mica eyepiece. Also, like the civilian duty respirator, the mask has a flutter valve exit hole above the filter. Next to the box is a pair of military respirator spectacles and their case. These have 'arms' made from flexible steel strip, designed to fit snugly under the mask, ensuring a gas tight fit. By September 1939, some 38 million gas masks had been distributed to British families.

> **Like the new Cenotaph, the Edith Cavell Monument is in St Martin's Place, off London's Trafalgar Square. It was unveiled by Queen Alexandra in 1920 and became a very popular subject for crested ware manufacturers in the immediate post-war years.**

Hartlepool, Margate or Weston-super-Mare. By 1914 four manufacturers in particular, Goss, Carlton, Shelley and Arcadian, had cornered the British market. The Goss pottery in Stoke-on-Trent, established by William Henry Goss, who had studied at the London School of Art and Design, was perhaps the most successful.

During the conflict, those who kept the home fires burning bought china battleships, monoplanes, airships, tanks, lorries, steel helmets, field artillery and a host of other items as patriotic souvenirs. Early in the Firt World War the most popular crested war models were those issued to signify British indignation at German atrocities such as the invasion of neutral Belgium and the sinking of the passenger liner RMS *Lusitania*. A particularly popular model commemorated the execution of Edith Cavell, the British nurse tried by German court martial in Brussels for helping Allied soldiers trapped in enemy-occupied parts of Belgium to escape into neutral Holland. The coming of peace saw collectors opt for china horseshoes emblazoned with the flags of the victorious Allies. The completion of Sir Edwin Lutyens's Cenotaph in Whitehall, London, in 1919 was an obvious subject for post-war souvenirs almost every family having lost a loved one, friend or relative during the bloody four years of war.

The 'Dead Man's Penny' is not as common as cigarette cards, postcards and crested ware, but given the staggering number of British casualties during the First World War, is a particularly moving relic of this period.

Nearly a million men (908,371 to be precise) from Britain and its empire were killed during the First World War. The opening day of the Battle of the Somme in July 1916 saw the British Army suffer the worst day in its history, sustaining nearly 60,000 casualties. Between 4 August 1914 and 11 November 1918, a total of 573,507 men *from the United Kingdom alone* were killed in action or died from their wounds. The slaughter of 1916, when the volunteer battalions – the so-called 'pals battalions', with many of them recruited from individual neighbourhoods so that soldiers would go into battle with friends and acquaintances – were scythed down by enemy machine guns the moment they left the trenches, encouraged the Government to commission a more fitting memento for families of the fallen than the War Office telegram, which had previously been the only official token of recognition of such mortal sacrifice. In 1917, the Government announced a competition to design a suitable plaque, offering a prize of £250 for the winning design. Whilst there were 800 entries from all over the Empire, and even from the troops on the Western Front, Mr E. Carter Preston of Liverpool, England, was the eventual winner. This winning design comprised a 12cm disc cast in

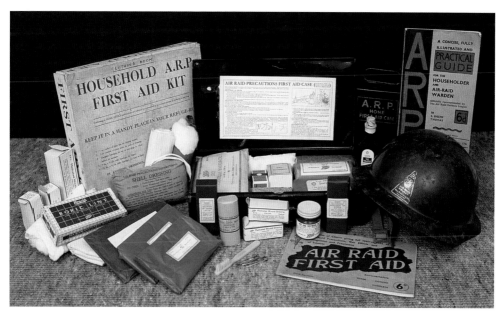

An arrangement of household ARP items, including two examples of the Boots ARP Home First Aid Case and contents; a Home Office approved Household ARP First Aid Kit ('Conforming to Home Office specifications and sufficient for a household of six to seven persons all sheltering in one room.'); a privately purchased air raid helmet, manufactured by Head Protectors Ltd of Grimsby, and a selection of period instructional pamphlets.

bronze gunmetal, which incorporated an image of Britannia and a lion, two dolphins representing Britain's sea power and the emblem of Imperial Germany's Eagle being torn to pieces by another lion. Britannia is holding an oak spray with leaves and acorns. Beneath this was a rectangular tablet where the deceased individual's name was cast into the plaque. No rank was given as it was intended to show equality in their sacrifice. On the outer edge of the disc were the words: 'He died for freedom and honour'. A parchment scroll measuring 27cm x 17cm and headed by the Royal Coat of Arms accompanied the plaque. Written in gothic script, the following passage accompanied individual plaques that were packaged in stiff cardboard wrapping and folded like an envelope before being sent to the next of kin: 'He whom this scroll commemorates was numbered among those who, at the call of King and Country, left all that was dear to them, endured hardness, faced danger, and finally passed out of sight of men by

WWII British air raid warden's whistle and chain. Manufactured in Birmingham and clearly marked 'ARP', when it was blown its sound was often followed by the barked instruction of 'Put that light out!'

the path of duty and self-sacrifice, giving up their own lives that others may live in freedom. Let those who come after see to it that his name be not forgotten.' Beneath this passage, written in the same style, was the name, rank and service details of the deceased. To accompany the scroll, again in gothic script, was a personal message from King George V: 'I join with my grateful people in sending you this memorial of a brave life given for others in the First World War. George R I.' Production of the plaques and scrolls began in 1919, with approximately 1,150,000 issued.

It might surprise some readers to discover that one popular Home Front collectable from the First World War period wasn't made in a British pottery or forge, or fashioned as 'trench art' from bullet and shell cases by soldiers enduring the muddy boredom between each successive big push. In fact, one particularly interesting collectable started life at Germany's Zeppelin plant in Friedrichshafen.

Although special gas masks were produced for the smaller heads of children (quickly Christened 'Mickey Mouse Masks' because of their prominent, snout-like filter canister), babies presented a much more difficult problem. The solution took the form of an all-encompassing hood covering the baby, which was secured neatly around the top of the infant's legs. As long as the parent remained uninjured, precious air could be pumped into the hood by means of the attached concertina bellows.

On the night of 2/3 September 1916, over Cuffley, Hertfordshire, Lieutenant William Leefe Robinson, flying a converted B.E.2c night fighter, earned the honour, and a VC, earned the honour of being the first RFC pilot to down an enemy airship, as well as bein awarded the VC. This was a huge achievement and the event was treated as a spectacular success (despite the fact that the fifteen other Zeppelins taking part in the raid returned to Germany unscathed). What better use for the wreckage than to cut it up and parcel up small components of the Kaiser's dreaded gasbag as souvenirs to be sold in support of the war effort? By war's end more then fifty Zeppelins had been shot down over Britain. Considering this amount, and the quantity of aluminium used to construct their filigree skeletons, it is perhaps no surprise that numerous relics from the earliest period of aerial warfare survive to be enjoyed by collectors today.

Naturally, today the majority of Home Front collectables available to enthusiasts come from the Second World War period. But chasing collectables dating specifically to the British Home Front for example, during the Second World War, is trickier than one might think. This is because that although Britain declared war on Germany on 3 September 1939, the nation had anticipated war with Hitler since the mid-1930s.

In 1919 German military aviation was specifically forbidden by the Treaty of Versailles

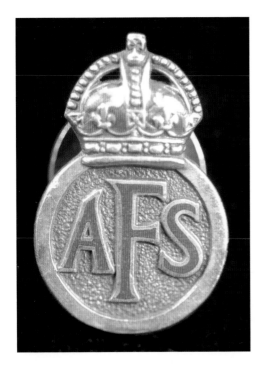

Enamel Auxiliary Fire Service (AFS) 'sweetheart' broach. Enormously popular, such badges were generally worn by loved ones to show support for either the branch of the armed forces or, as in this case, the auxiliary or volunteer service in which their beloved served.

but in February 1935 Adolf Hitler ordered Hermann Goering to establish the Luftwaffe. In March 1936 German troops marched into the demilitarized zone of the Rhineland and the Fuhrer began to systematically ignore the treaties that limited the size of Germany's armed forces, and in contravention of international agreement was in fact rapidly increasing the size of his army, navy and brand new air force. It didn't stop here for in March 1938 German troops marched

This classic silver ARP badge was manufactured by the thousand and widely distributed. Examples can still be readily discovered amongst collections of bric-a-brac.

Distinctive hallmarks on the reverse of the silver badge given to wartime ARP personnel and worn on their lapels when off duty. These badges are quite common but the novice might not realize that they are solid silver!

into Austria, Hitler's birthplace, declaring *Anschluss* (union) with that independent nation. Throughout the summer of 1938 the Nazis whipped up national fervour amongst German descendants living in the bordering Sudeten region of Czechoslovakia, demanding that this region be ceded to the Reich. At the infamous Munich Conference in September 1938, British Prime Minister Neville Chamberlain and others signed a treaty that gave Hitler what he wanted. Soon after this Germany quietly occupied the rest of Czechoslovakia and very shortly a sovereign state that had only existed from October 1918, when it declared its independence from the Austro-Hungarian Empire, effectively ceased to exist. As can be imagined, throughout the year 1938, especially, most people in Britain, including the Government, expected war with Germany at any moment. As a result, a large amount of material to do with air raid precautions (ARP), particularly the threat of chemical attack (poison gas) from the air, was either officially distributed to provide civilians with information about what to expect in the event of total war, or could be purchased privately. Publishers had a field day and a startling

After one of the Government's early wartime posters backfired (ordinary people thought that that the 'Us' in the strapline '*Your* Courage, *Your* Cheerfulness, *Your* Resolution Will Bring Us Victory' suggested that ordinary people were expected to sacrifice their efforts for the ruling classes) every effort was made to tell workers and non-combatants that we were all in it together, as these five cards explain.

Though formed in the early 1930s, the members of the Crazy Gang (Bud Flanagan, Chesney Allen, Jimmy Nervo, Teddy Knox, Charlie Naughton and Jimmy Gold) kept the British public entertained during WWII on the radio and in a series of films.

number of books and pamphlets telling ordinary people what to do, even a number that could be privately purchased by reservists in the territorials, flooded the market.

So beware, something sold as having Second World War provenance may, in fact, date from the pre-war years when many assumed the worst. Similarly, some of the measures restricting civil liberties, most notably rationing, remained in place for some years after the Second World War. Check the dates on ration books – the end of all food rationing did not arrive until July 1954! Britain's ARP movement can actually trace its origins to 1924, when a government committee produced figures estimating that in London there would be 9,000 casualties in the first two days of an air attack and then a continuing rate of 17,500 casualties a week. With the development of the Civil Defence (CD) service in 1941, the main function of the ARP fell within the remit of this organization and although disbanded in 1946, the functions of the ARP were

NAZI Volkssturm armband. The Volkssturm were the Third Reich's equivalent of Britain's Home Guard and by the war's end comprised mostly boys and old men fighting desperately amongst the rubble of a ruined Germany.

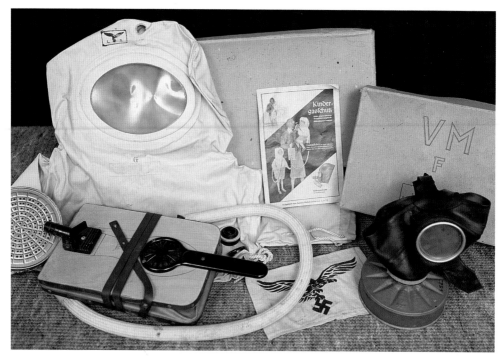

A selection of German WWII Luftschutz (ARP) items. In the picture from the left is an ultra-rare mint and boxed German babies' respirator (notice the Luftschutz emblem printed above the visor and the surviving instruction leaflet showing the equipment in operation); a Luftschutz armband to be worn in conjunction with the helmet (shown elsewhere in this book) and a civilian respirator.

Very rare early-war German toy Heinkel He 111 bomber. Manufactured by the famous firm of Lehmann, this tinplate toy is all the more remarkable for being complete with its original box and accessories. We know it's an early toy because the machine carries the markings and camouflage of the Luftwaffe's Kondo Legion which supported Franco's nationalist armies during the Spanish Civil War.

WWII German magnesium 'Electron' incendiary – the notoriously effective 'Firebomb Fritz'. Designed to be dropped in large quantities over urban areas to create uncontrollable firestorms, they detonated on impact, igniting a magnesium compound that rapidly burned white-hot and was difficult to extinguish. Notorious for their habit of crashing through roof tiles and within consumable timber joists, not all of them detonated, however. 'Duds', often without their delicate aluminium tailfins, became sought-after schoolboy souvenirs. A 'Firex' (fire extinguishing grenade) is also shown. When thrown at the base of a fire the grenade smashed and the carbon-tetrachloride within inhibited combustion.

Hitler Youth bronze sports award pin. *Deutsches Jungvolk Leistungsabzeichen* (German Young Person's Performance Badge). This lapel pin is a small version of a much larger award. This, one of the author's most cherished possessions, was given to him by his good friend Herb Schmitz, who was forced to part with most of the trophies he won at school in return for food from occupying GIs.

revived as part of the Civil Defence Corps formed in 1949. So again, the novice must err on the side of caution; a lot of ARP and CD material claimed as being of Second World War origin in fact dates from the days of post-war nuclear paranoia of the Cold War period.

The variety of surviving authentic Second World War Home Front collectable material is staggering. Ranging from vintage ration books, children's evacuation labels, aircraft recognition booklets and patriotic sheet music to specially hooded domestic ARP lamps with concealed bulbs covered by a sloping cowl that directed the light to the ground if held upright (sturdier versions of these were produced for ARP wardens and policemen), special metal baffles to be fitted on car headlights, which emitted a narrow beam of

Washboard and two boxes of wartime soap powder. The packet of Rinso provided specific wartime instructions and on the carton of Oxydol, a message told purchasers that because less cardboard was used in its construction, buying the product amounted to 'Two More Nails in Hitler's Coffin!'

illumination, and even original blackout material used to prevent household light escaping through gaps in curtains, the choice is bountiful.

Many people associate Second World War collectables purely with the military but those items specific to civilians who were 'doing their bit' either at home or as part of their National Service after a day's work are, in my opinion, far more interesting. The importance of this period in Britain's history is confirmed, if confirmation was necessary

A fine selection of wartime William Britain toy soldiers, AA guns, searchlights and range calculators. The tiny figure in the left foreground is an observer reclined in a specially designed chair.

A rather macabre set of toy figures, clad in decontamination gear. Manufactured by the well-known toy soldier manufacturer Taylor & Barrett, this rare set is redolent of the anxiety about chemical warfare, which even found its way into 1930s' toy boxes.

(ask anyone who lived through the Blitz) by the fact that the subject is currently covered by the British national curriculum. At the time of writing, school children between the ages of eight and eleven (Key Stage 2) are encouraged to learn about evacuation, rationing, the role of women and the Home Guard, among other Second World War topics.

Learning from their experiences during the 1914–1918 conflict, from 1939–1945, to a greater or lesser degree, the authorities of every combatant nation introduced a variety of voluntary or compulsory terms of engagement in National Service which saw civilians enrolled into a wide range of activities to support the war effort. Those either too young or too old for conscription, or kept at home in reserved occupations, were encouraged to join their nations' equivalent of the Home Guard (Germany – Volkssturm) or ARP (Luftschutz).

In the age before email and mobile phones, and when communication relied on a very vulnerable public telephone system operated by the GPO (General Post Office), thousands of youngsters were engaged as bicycle messengers, this being the only reliable way of communicating important information once the existing infrastructure had been damaged by the Blitz. In fact it seems that British youngsters were actually directly involved in collecting military objects quite early on in the war and I'm not talking about badges and other insignia. My good friend Peter Osborne was eight when the war started. Evacuated during the 'phoney war', when nothing much seemed to happen, like thousands of other children in 1940 he returned to his family home. Peter lived in Peckham, South London. His father, an asthmatic and unfit for military service, nevertheless did his bit in the ARP. Like all his other school friends, Peter collected the detritus that littered the local streets the morning after an air raid. He recalls: 'The streets were full of shell splinters, bits of bombs and pieces of shrapnel and like all the other

WWII period Dinky Toys aircraft. The trade pack contains six delightful miniature Bristol Blenheim fighter bombers and in the foreground is a Fairey Battle light bomber and a Supermarine Spitfire fighter.

boys, on the way to school I picked up every bit I could. Taking them in to school we all compared our little treasures, competing to see who had the best collection. The winner was the one with the biggest piece. For several weeks I was king of the heap because I had a 9-inch-long lump of jagged metal. "Cor! Look what Ginger's got" my friends would say. That is until a few weeks later when another boy came in with an even bigger lump.' Peter went on to tell me that shell splinters were, as their name suggests, very sharp and jagged. They were still capable of doing damage long after being dropped from the Heinkels and Dorniers that had passed thousands of feet over head. Woe betides the boy who dropped a heavy iron shard on his foot.

Briefly, while staying on the same theme, Peter told me that despite his father dealing with the effects of German air raids first hand in the ARP, the only time he really heard his dad angrily curse the enemy was when a stray shell splinter had a direct effect on his ablutions. Like most other working-class families at the time, Peter's house was devoid of a bathroom and only had cold running water. Bathing required both the zinc bath and domestic copper to be brought into the house. The copper was then filled with water and placed on a gas ring to heat it before emptying it by turning on its tap and filling the bath. 'The morning after one particularly heavy raid, when the ack-ack guns were blasting away all night, my father discovered a hole punched neatly through the lid of the copper with another

'Boys! Just the book you've been looking for,' claimed this wartime classic *Aeroplane* drawing book.

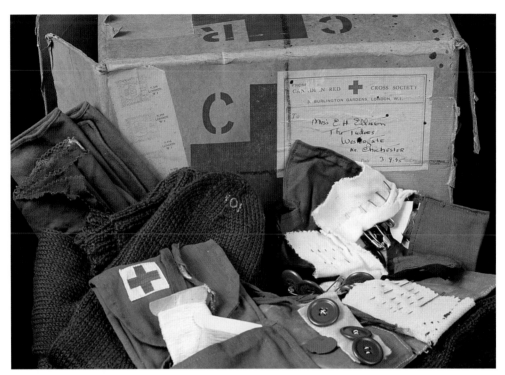

Contents of a 1945-vintage Canadian Red Cross parcel destined for an Allied prisoner of war (POW). An incredibly rare survivor, full of consumable materials produced during the height of the austerity period. The comforts and food items come from both Canada and the US.

Buffs sweetheart brooch. This is a nice example of an enamel badge fixed to a mother-of-pearl backing. In recent years the value of sweetheart badges of all types has soared.

torn through the bottom. Lifting the copper revealed the culprit another lump of German metal. 'I can remember my dad going apoplectic with fury – cursing the Hun for robbing the family of their bath!' remembered Peter with a smile.

Women and children, men either too old or too young for military service, together with those male workers, especially farmers and skilled factory workers kept at home in 'reserved occupations', endured the terrors of the Blitz, the privations of rationing and the restrictions caused by the blackout as best they could. Naturally, the majority of household items in use during wartime were basically the same as those employed

War was never far away from civilians –
even when they were playing cribbage at
home. This Lee-Enfield .303 rifle butt is
also decorated with the cap badge of the
Buffs, the East Kent Regiment.

in peacetime – it was just that
replacements for commonplace
items became harder to find and
'frivolous' items such as stockings
and cosmetics became expensive
and could often only be obtained illicitly on the black market. It was a time of 'make do
and mend'. Women took down their old curtains and rather than disposing of them, cut
them up to make skirts and dresses. The wool from unwanted jumpers was unravelled
and knitted into something else. Because make-up and stockings were so hard to come
by, some girls drew a line down the back of each leg with an eye pencil and pretended
they were wearing stockings. Others used gravy browning to dye their legs but on a hot
day this apparently attracted flies! Patches were sewn onto the bottoms of short trousers
to breathe new life into schoolboys' clothes and even underwear was repaired. Mothers

ARP inert training model of the Luftwaffe's
infamous 'butterfly bomb' (Sprengbombe
Dickwandig 2kg or SD2), the 2kg anti-
personnel aerial mine that would drop, liked the
'winged' seeds of a sycamore tree once its
spring-loaded wings flipped out. The turning
wings rotated a spindle connected to the fuse,
with the result that many of these nasty
bomblets were often left primed and hanging in
tree branches waiting to be dislodged, with
dangerous consequences, by a gust of wind or
the prodding stick of an over-inquisitive child.

were encouraged to knit socks with double
yarn on the toes and heels, and to darn
these areas on old socks if they were worn.
Bed sheets that had become thin in the
middle were cut in half and the former
outer sides were sewn together to make a
stronger replacement, with the worn
patches on the edges being tucked under
the mattress. A seam down the middle of a
sheet might be uncomfortable but it was
better than going without one at all.
Sewing patterns were published that used
the least fabric possible to make a new
garment, and skirts were shorter and
slimmer to save fabric. Full skirts or those
with numerous pleats were a thing of the
past. Fabric was snipped from the tail of
men's shirts to repair frayed collars and
cuffs were made so that when frayed, the
tatty edge could be folded up onto the
inside and hidden. The turn-ups on men's
trousers were folded so that when they

Thousands of ARP and CD personnel were involved in fire watching, spotting the fall of incendiaries in an effort to direct fire services to the most troublesome blazes. Employees in many firms and factories also volunteered for such duties and numerous badges, such as the example shown here, were manufactured so that those who volunteered for such work could be identified when relaxing in 'civvies'.

The War Illustrated (11 October 1940), edited by Sir John Hammerton, who worked closely with Alfred Harmsworth, 1st Viscount Northcliffe, the British newspaper and publishing magnate whose company Amalgamated Press founded the *Daily Mirror* in 1903 and rescued *The Observer* and *The Times* when they were both in financial difficulty a few years later.

frayed the garment looked marginally better. Shoe polish wasn't available so people were advised to cut a potato in half and use that to bring a shine to their shoes. And so on and so on …

Because it was positively dangerous to go out in the blackout – you might get caught in the middle of an air raid or knocked over by a vehicle that, because its headlights

Perhaps not surprisingly for a nation that brought you 78rpm records of classics such as *Bomben auf Engelland* (*Bombs on England*) and *Wir Fahren Gegen Engelland* (*We Journey Against England*), Nazi Germany's youngsters supplemented their traditional board games with some more militaristic table-top activities. In one version of bagatelle named 'Bombers over England', children as young as four were encouraged to blow up settlements by firing a spring-driven ball onto a board featuring a map of Britain and the tip of Northern Europe. Players were awarded a maximum 100 points for landing on London, while Liverpool was worth forty.

Run Rabbit Run! sheet music. Written for Noel Gay's show *The Little Dog Laughed*, which opened on 11 October 1939, the song became especially popular after Flanagan and Allen changed the lyrics to poke fun at the Germans and specifically Hitler (hence: *Run Adolf, Run Adolf, Run, Run, Run*).

WWII period HMS *Ajax* commemorative ceramic cup. Made famous for her part in the Battle of the River Plate on 13 December 1939, when, together with HMS *Exeter* and HMS *Achilles*, HMS *Ajax* took part in Britain's first victory of WWII – the sinking of the German pocket battleship *Admiral Graf Spee*.

were so carefully shielded, was barely discernible in the gloom – most people made the most of staying at home. The radio proved a most welcome companion and popular shows like *It's That Man Again* (*ITMA*) starring Tommy Handley and featuring a host of memorable characters such as Mrs Mopp and Colonel Chinstrap, are alleged to have sustained the war effort on the Home Front. Interestingly the title *ITMA* was first coined by Herbert Smith 'Bert' Gunn, a journalist with the *Daily Express* who repeatedly used it in his pre-war articles when referring to the increasingly alarming, and sometimes comical, activities of Adolf Hitler during the so called 'phoney war'. Now you know.

When not listening to the radio or darning socks, civilians on the Home Front of all the European belligerents spent a lot of time playing games. Some clever people probably multi-tasked and combined all three. In Britain popular games included all the classics such as chess, snakes and ladders and ludo. Card games of all sorts were enormously popular and the plethora of aircraft recognition cards that came onto the market added a new twist to the genre while teaching civilians how to distinguish an RAF Wellington bomber from a Luftwaffe Ju88.

Cigarette cards were an enormously popular premium at a time when so much of the population smoked. This very popular ARP set from W.D. & H.O. Wills provides a fascinating window into a time that is thankfully far behind us. The cards of highest value are the ones in mint condition and, disappointingly, not glued into an album, however well affixed.

Naturally, German civilians shared many of the experiences of their British counterparts. And, arguably, as the war progressed they suffered even greater privations, imbibing acorn (*ersatz*) coffee and slicing bread made from silage and weeds.

On the playing board of another game, which included cellulose playing pieces representing Luftwaffe aircraft and Kriegsmarine warships, a map of Europe enabled youngsters to range far and wide. Players were penalized and lost points if they hit 'Allied' cities such as Brussels and

Wartime petrol coupon dating from September 1940. Petrol was the first commodity to be rationed and its purchase was restricted from 16 September 1939.

This rather innocuous looking object fascinates me. A Boy Scout woggle (nice segue from the piece in the introduction about Baden-Powell in the Transvaal eh?) belonging to Allan Parker, the maternal grandfather of a friend and colleague of mine, Duncan Hussey. Manufactured from lightweight aluminium, it was made while Mr Parker worked as a toolmaker at de Havilland's in Hatfield, during WWII. It was fashioned from a section of the tubular framework of the German airship *SL11*, which Lieutenant W. Leefe Robinson shot down on 3 September 1916 above nearby Cuffley. Anne Parker, Duncan's mother, remembers that her father, a Scout leader in St Albans, ended up with a unique means of securing his neckerchief. This fastening was then passed on to his grandson generations later, when it was the youngster's turn to join the Boy Scouts. 'I felt proud to use that rather than the usual coloured plastic one,' Duncan told me.

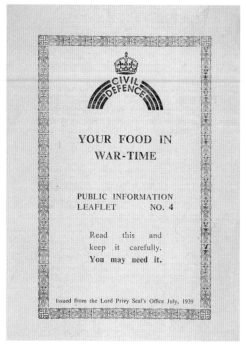

'Your Food In Wartime' – the seventh in a pretty comprehensive series of Civil Defence leaflets, which dropped through the letterboxes of home owners in Britain during WWII, designed to tell them everything they needed to do to cope with the exigencies of total war.

Amsterdam. There was also a version of Snakes and Ladders in which battleships sailed from Germany to England and back, attacking targets of opportunity along the way.

Because of regular aerial bombing, for the first time civilians in the British Isles and on continental Europe were frequently in the front line so it's hardly surprising that after enduring endless nights of bombing from an often unseen enemy, ordinary, previously quite decent people, soon developed a hard and apparently unfeeling exterior. The British gave as good as they got and themselves produced a number of quite disrespectful, to say the least, anti-German board games. Some were more overtly political than others.

Several dartboards used pictures of infamous political figures as targets. The 'Plonk' dartboard depicted German Foreign Minister Ribbentrop with a snake's body and showed Goering brandishing a caveman club. As you might expect, a caricature of Hitler

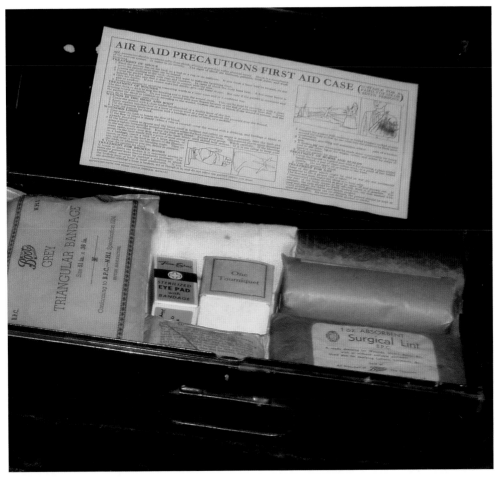

Contents of a Boots the Chemist home ARP first aid kit. This was typical of the wide variety of commercially produced outfits that could be purchased on the high street.

is the bullseye, with a gaping black mouth and marked for 100 points. Similarly, the 'Allies Dart Game' featured a large picture of Hitler's face, and points were scored depending on where the dart landed. A direct hit on Hitler's moustache, for example, scored you fifty points. 'Decorate Goering – A Party Game', was based on the classic children's game 'Pin theTail on the Donkey'. Like its more innocuous counterpart, players were blindfolded, but rather than abusing the poor donkey they had to pin medals on Goering's tunic.

It has to be said that on both sides that what boys' toys were available – and these were only really common during the early war years – were often very militaristic. With its tradition of toy making and especially with model soldiers and tinplate novelties, Nuremberg's toy manufactures produced a steady stream of toy soldiers, tanks, warships and aircraft. Brands such as Elastolin, a trademark used by O. & M. Hausser, famous for its unique composite figures, equipped toy armies with infantrymen, sentry boxes, anti-tank obstacles and heavy machinegunners. Lehmann, who specialized in some of the finest tinplate work, manufactured an exquisite series of miniature Heinkel bombers and monoplane fighters. Again, these are based on pre-war aircraft types that remained available to the toy trade until stocks ran out. Today, examples of such tinplate miniatures can still be found but expect to pay between £300 and £800 depending on the condition of the tinplate item and its packaging. Similarly, Elastolin figures are still quite common, as being cheap and manufactured from little more than a sawdust-and-glue combination, they were produced in their millions. Again, condition will dictate price. When studying an original Elastolin figure check to see if any of the wire armature, upon which the figure was assembled, is poking through a component part such as an arm or leg – or, most commonly of all, is revealed as the basis of a gun barrel. As soon as they are cracked or broken Elastolin figures become very fragile indeed.

Probably the most famous British equivalent to Germany's Elastolin figures are those produced by William Britain, who in 1893 invented the process of hollow casting in lead

Defence Medal (1939–45) awarded for non-operational service, including those service personnel working in headquarters, on training bases and airfields and members of the Home Guard. Home Guard service counts between the dates of 14 May 1940 and 31 December 1944. The medal features the uncrowned head of King George VI and, on the reverse, the Royal Crown resting on an oak tree and two lions above the words 'The Defence Medal'. The flame colour in the centre of the ribbon is flanked by stripes of green to symbolize enemy attacks on Britain's 'green and pleasant land', with narrow black stripes to represent the blackout. These medals aren't that uncommon but it's not that easy to find one complete with its original box and certificate.

Imposed on 1 September 1939, blackout regulations caused more British fatalities during the first months of WWII than enemy action. To prevent enemy bomber pilots navigating by means of recognizing conurbations and highways, windows and doors were required to be covered at night with heavy curtains or cardboard, and street lights were switched off. Motorcar headlights were dimmed by the addition of headlight baffles, which directed what little light escaped downward.

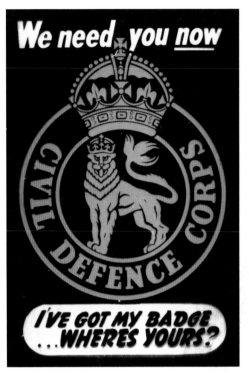

Post-WWII government poster urging civilians to join the Civil Defence Corps, the volunteer organization established in Great Britain in 1949 to take control in the aftermath of a nuclear attack. It wasn't stood down until 1968.

and revolutionized the production of toy soldiers. Made of metal, Britain's soldiers are far more robust than Germany's composite equivalent and therefore survive in much larger quantities. Finding early examples of unshipped figures or sets intact in their original boxes is the goal of every collector – finding them at a bargain price is the enthusiast's dream and sometimes, just sometimes, such items can be purchased for a song.

When they were demobbed from the First World War Fred G. Taylor and his brother-in-law, A.R. Barrett (who had been a lead caster at William Britain Junior before 1914) founded their own company, Taylor & Barrett, which existed from 1920 until 1941 in London's Holloway. Famous for some of their delightful pre-war 'Munich Crisis' period figure sets showing decontamination crews clad in anti-gas overalls and protective helmets, like early Britain's figures, Taylor & Barrett originals command a premium price.

Interestingly, following the awful carnage of the First World War and in tune with the anti-war *zeitgeist* of the post-war period, in the 1920s Britain decided to manufacture figures other than soldiers' tanks and guns, and their much more pacific farming series, which endures to this day, was born.

Other notable British manufacturers of toys popular during wartime included Frank Hornby's giant Dinky Toys range, which in 1938 introduced a number of new military vehicles. Painted dark olive green, the range featured tanks, an Austin 7 staff car, a Jeep, a six-wheeled passenger truck, a troop carrier, a searchlight truck, and a light Dragon tractor towing a field gun. Production of the first series of these new toys ceased in 1940, although some, such as No. 161, an 'Anti-Aircraft Gun' and No. Dinky 151a 'Medium Tank' had proved so popular they were manufactured again between 1946 and 1948. Both civilian and military aircraft were Dinky subjects and between 1939 and 1941 a model Spitfire was sold in a special presentation box in support of the Spitfire Fund in order to raise money for the production of this outstanding monoplane fighter.

Australian Women's Land Army cloth patch. Modelled on Britain's organisation, the Australian Women's Land Army was formed on 27 July 1942, the threat from Japan seeing male agricultural labour drafted into the Australian military with women engaged to make up the shortfall on the land.

Naturally, model aircraft were particularly popular. Spitfire and Hurricanes caused a sensation barely a generation or two since man had first managed powered flight. Fortunately. another famous company, FROG, succeeded in meeting youngsters' demands for miniature-scale replicas of all the newest aircraft around. Founded in 1931 by Charles Wilmot and Joe Mansour, International Model Aircraft Ltd (IMA) originally used the FROG brand name (said to stand for 'Flies Right Off the Ground') for its rubber band-powered flying model aircraft. But after they joined forces with the huge Lines Bros concern (the UK's largest toy manufacturer) in 1932, they decided to produce a range of non-flying plastic model construction kits. Fittingly known by the brand name 'Penguin' (a non-flying bird), by 1936 a range of 1:72 scale aircraft models, moulded in cellulose acetate, was launched, having the honour of being the world's first true plastic model construction kits. By 1938, Hurricanes, Spitfires and even a giant Empire flying boat were available for eager enthusiasts who each waited the next exciting release.

Naturally, production of kits ceased during the Second World War and IMA patriotically went on to produce flying models for target purposes so that the growing number of anti-aircraft gunners had something to practise with. They also used their skills to manufacture numerous 1:72 scale aircraft recognition models so that regular soldiers, Home Guard volunteers and ARP wardens could memorize the silhouettes of all types of aircraft. It was found that being able to study a model in 3D was far superior to simply memorizing the traditional three-view silhouettes in aircraft recognition manuals or on posters. Numerous other British manufacturers produced patriotic 'war toys' during the early part of the Second World War. Notable amongst these are the firm of Astra (famous for their model searchlights and AA guns), Charbens and Johillco for toy soldiers, and Crescent for cheaper die-cast vehicles and novelties.

Chapter 6

Printed Material and Ephemera

If I'm being honest, to me, by far the most interesting items I have collected over the years aren't materially that impressive. My Luftwaffe dagger, RAF Type B flying helmet, Lehmann tinplate Heinkel or set of Taylor & Barrett ARP figures might be where the money's at and, whether they like it are not, are part of my daughters' meagre inheritance. But they don't really do very much for me. On the contrary, I get much more pleasure and hours of enjoyment from many of the items that are the least valuable in my collection: the books, magazines and numerous instruction leaflets, manuals and

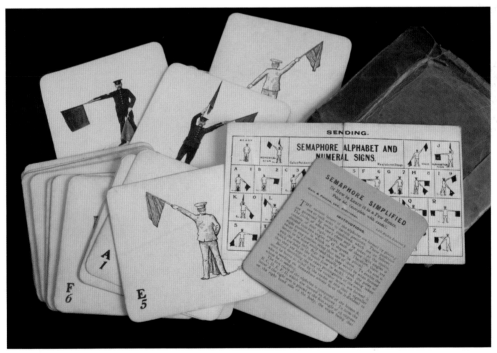

Set of WWI *Semaphore Simplified* cards by that most prolific of instructional publishers, Gale & Polden. The A-Z cards would, claimed the instructions, allow the dedicated student to 'master the cards in a matter of hours'. In the days before reliable radio communications, semaphore signalling was of vital importance. It might surprise many readers to learn that semaphore is still in use today, and is especially useful at sea during ship-to-ship refuelling operations, for example.

hand books that are produced by government and the military to tell soldiers and civilians what to do and when to do it during wartime.

The authors and publishers of most of what was produced – much of it, such as the various invasion warnings distributed throughout Britain in 1940 produced in emergency – probably never expected their efforts to survive much beyond the immediate period they were made. Indeed, the dictionary definition of ephemera is 'items designed to last only for a short period, such as programmes or posters'.

In my opinion handbills entitled 'Advising the Public in the Event of Invasion' delivered to anxious citizens following the debacle of Dunkirk, or 'A Last Appeal to Reason by Adolf Hitler', which the Luftwaffe dropped over England shortly afterwards, are of enormous value that far exceeds their monetary worth. For far too long such items of printed matter have been overlooked in favour of Irvin flying jackets and Wehrmacht *Stahlhelms*.

For collectors of militaria, 'ephemera' covers a slightly wider range of items including magazines, newspapers – books, even. In wartime, the numerous official instructions

'*In Gedanken bei dir*,'or 'Thinking of you.' German postcard from 1914. This, and the adjacent British postcard from the same period, is emblematic of the enthusiasm and naivety that carried each protagonist to the precipice and beyond at the outbreak of WWI.

'Bravo! Territorials.' Patriotic British postcard from 1914. 'There's none can say you lag. In answering your Country's call to rally round the flag.' The similarity between this card and the German one is strikingly poignant. Little did they know …

By Christmas 1914, the British Army had expanded from 200,000 men to more than a million. The war that was to be 'over by Christmas' certainly wasn't, but at least those thousands of troops enduring a bitter winter in the trenches enjoyed one comfort from home – Princess Mary's Christmas gift tin. (Some also had the pleasure of a football game with the enemy during the famous, unofficial, truce on 25 December.) Created under the stewardship of the 17-year-old daughter of King George V and Queen Mary, this most welcome package, a 'gift from the nation', contained a Christmas card, cigarettes and tobacco (non-smokers and certain dominion troops received confectionary). These tins aren't that uncommon but finding an example like the one shown here, complete with its contents, commands a premium price.

and notices distributed amongst the civilian population, together with countless service handbooks, supplements and training manuals, are also ephemeral in nature. Mass-produced ephemeral material wasn't much in evidence before theIndustrial Revolution and most notably the introduction of cheap high-speed lithographic printing. Whilst there are still some First World War gems like aircraft spotters' guides illustrating the silhouettes of not only enemy biplanes, but Zeppelin airships, or instructions telling Kitchener's 'Old Contemptibles' how to behave when in contact with French civilians for example, these pieces are few and far between.

Examples of First World War ephemera, whether produced by the Allies or Central Powers, are not far off a hundred years old. Being generally cheaply produced, the paper used was often of low quality. Indeed, paper-manufacturing technology in the early twentieth century was still in its infancy, the bleaches used to clean the pulp often contributing to early deterioration. In fact, even the best of surviving First World War printed material is likely to be yellowed and brittle.

Although there are collections of First World War ephemera, as there are from the inter-war years (the fabled 'goolie chits' carried by RAF pilots flying along the North West Frontier, designed to encourage tribespeople to return downed aviators intact in return for a reward, being very collectable!) and post-Second World War items (Korean, Vietnam and Gulf War propaganda pieces being top of the list), it has to be said that most collectors seek items from the Second World War. Many of the official orders and training supplements were produced in emergency. Government instructions to 'Stay Put!' or how to achieve 'Beating the Invader' were hurriedly produced because of the prospect of a Nazi invasion in 1940. Manuals for the P17, Springfield rifle, purchased from storage in the America for distribution to the Home Guard, were like the .300 calibre rifle (British service rifles were .303) – short-lived. These items, like instructions for the Local Defence Volunteers (LDV), regarding the ill-fated sound locators, the predecessor and possible cover ruse for RADAR, were produced in relatively small numbers and were around for a short time, so they are quite rare.

One of the criticisms frequently levelled at collectors and hobbyists in general is that they tend to be somewhat myopic, unable to grasp the complete picture. It's true that

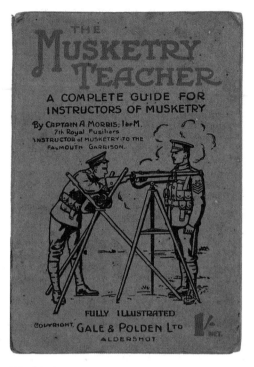

The Musketry Teacher. Publisher Gale & Polden began life located near Brompton Barracks, close to the naval base in Chatham, Kent. Consequently, they quickly obtained a range of government contracts and by the end of the nineteenth century had moved to Aldershot to be even closer to the heart of Britain's military establishment. In 1916 they were even granted a Royal Warrant for producing Queen Mary's Christmas card to the forces. As part of a major printing acquisition the late Robert Maxwell gained control of Gale & Polden in 1981, subsuming in it within his British Printing Corporation (BPC).

enthusiasts can be short-sighted, perhaps unable to see the passion in its then contemporary context and … getting things out of proportion. Well, one way of making sense of a Second World War badge or uniform collection is to study the plethora of printed material produced alongside such items. Only by understanding field service regulations will an enthusiast truly appreciate the sense behind military procedure. A Royal Engineer's field service manual explains the relevance of the various trades and skills depicted in cloth and metal insignia, which combine to create a modern mechanized army. Flicking through a surviving Wills ARP cigarette card album encourages a better

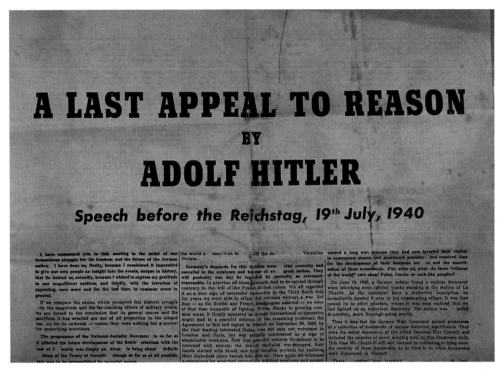

By the summer of 1940, Britain was the only European country still at war with the all-conquering Nazis. Invasion appeared imminent and although it was not part of his original plan, Hitler was preparing for the eventuality of a landing in England. This is a very rare surviving example of the text to the Führer's famous 'Last Appeal To Reason' speech to the Reichstag on 19 July 1940, which was translated into English and reproduced as a newsprint broadsheet. However, any hopes the Führer might have entertained that his olive branch would encourage the British to sue for peace were soon dispelled. Although thousands of copies were dropped from the bomb bays of Luftwaffe war planes over the British Isles, they were poorly received. The British press had a great time making fun of the Nazi communiqué and many British householders simply used the broadsheets as spare lavatory paper!

understanding of the numerous civil defence and auxiliary organizations supplementing the regular forces during the Blitz.

Collecting wartime ephemera has advantages beyond the educational, of course. Storing dozens of old leaflets and magazines is considerably easier than conserving combat gear like battledress blouses and greatcoats. Although the most collectable items of printed ephemera are those produced in limited numbers, many publications – most noticeably the famous His Majesty'sStationery Office (HMSO) series – were printed in quantity. Their very number means that a great deal have survived, are still affordable and can be found at boot sales and in charity shops for a few pounds. Indeed, it's worth snapping up originals. Since the fiftieth anniversary of the Second World War facsimiles have been produced by HMSO (Her Majesty's Stationery Office), a testament to their quality and desirability and an indication of demand – so why not own the original if you can?

Though much has been written about whether or not Hitler seriously considered invading Britain, this map is proof that some preparations, at least, were made in earnest. A very rare find, this is a small section of a large (8ft x 6ft) German *Unternehmen Seelöwe* (Operation Sealion) invasion map from 1940. Overall the map shows the likely invasion areas of Kent and Sussex. In fact, this map is an overprinted version of a British Ordnance Survey map – the all-conquering Führer clearly not worrying about the niceties of copyright infringement!

As is the general rule in Second World War militaria, objects related to the Third Reich are of highest value. This does not necessarily mean German-produced material, of course – although material that survived the destruction of Hitler's Germany is rarer than the proverbial hens' teeth.

The shock caused by Britain's declaration of war on 3 September 1939 was visceral. After such a long period of earnest appeasement the British felt duped by 'Herr Hitler' and much to the embarrassment of the far right, British publishers produced a flurry of satirical pamphlets, printed novelties and song sheets depicting the Führer in a satirical light. The words and music to Annette Mills's famous *Adolf* can still be found today. Featuring a photograph of popular comedian Arthur Askey, who recorded the ditty, the cover of this foolscap sized song sheet shows the Führer sprawled across 'Old Bill's' bended knee as Bruce Bairnsfather's famous First World War soldier Old Bill, wallops the Nazi with a hob nailed ammunition boot. Another satirical period publication that can still be found in second-hand bookshops is the *Daily Sketch* newspaper's war relief fundraiser *Struwelhitler*. Costing just 1s 6d (7p), this booklet was a parody of the famous German children's story *Struwelpeter*. *Adolf in Blunderland*, a less than subtle parody of

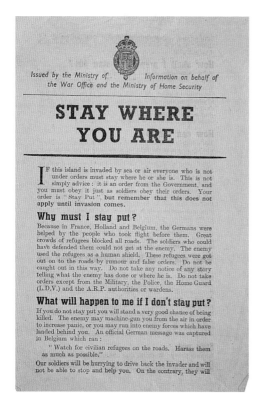

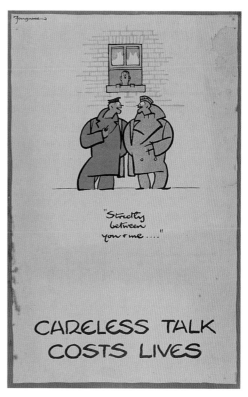

Stay Where You Are – British Government anti-invasion leaflet. Convinced that the success of Hitler's armies on the continent (France was overwhelmed in barely six weeks) was to a large part down to the fact that roads were blocked by refugees and signposts were removed by 'Fifth Columnists', when in fact the Allied defeat was brought about because of its own poor command and control, in the summer of 1940 the authorities decided it would be prudent to tell the British public to stay put in the event of a German landing.

Under the pen name 'Fougasse', which was a type of French mine, the cartoonist Cyril Bird (1887–1965) designed the famous series of 'Careless Talk Cost Lives' posters in 1939. In good condition these posters now command premium prices at auction.

Lewis Carroll's classic work about Alice, of course, was illustrated by Norman Mansbridge. It rather viscously portrayed Prime Minister Neville Chamberlain as the novel's blue, hookah-smoking caterpillar perched on a toadstool emblazoned with Hitler's conquests. Hitler was 'Alice'!

An area often overlooked by militaria collectors is that of wartime children's books. Lots of terrific examples survive – all ephemeral in nature because, like Richmal Crompton's *William and ARP* and *William the Dictator,* they were really only relevant during wartime. In fact, there were many short-lived developments during the Second World War, the impact of which, though brief, was sufficient for them to be immortalized in children's books and periodicals. A particular one was the barrage balloon, soon made redundant by technological advances in aerial warfare. In an effort to demystify these potential scary objects, they were humanized. Books like *Bulgy the Barrage Balloon*, *Boo-Boo the Barrage Balloon* and the more originally titled *Blossom the Brave Balloon* were illustrated with cheerful cartoons and accompanied by a narrative encouraging youngsters to bond with the tethered inflatables mushrooming above factories and dock installations.

With so many troops from overseas in Britain during the Second World War it's not surprising that an awful lot of published material was designed to help them integrate into a very different society from home. Alongside booklets advising troops from the United States and British Dominions about customs in what one humourist called *Occupied England*, there were numerous unofficial publications like *Got Any Gum Chum?* and *Where's the Garbage Can?* that attempted to bridge the gap between often quite disparate cultures.

Douglas Tempest (1887–1954) was another established cartoonist engaged in the war effort. 'What about your registration?' is a postcard from Bamforth & Co's Tempest Iddy series. Best known for their saucy seaside postcards, Yorkshire-based Bamforth's commissioned a series of patriotic designs. Encouraging the recipient to consider joining the ARP, this particular example was posted on 7 September 1939, only four days after the outbreak of WWII.

It's beyond the scope of this book to consider all ephemera worth collecting but enthusiasts might also choose to track down examples of surviving packaging. Soap powder boxes, like Oxydol, for example, carried patriotic messages. Oxydol's was: 'Two More Nails In Hitler's Coffin! – To save cardboard for the nation we have reduced the size of this packet. The cardboard saved from this packet is enough to make two cartridge wads. The weight of Oxydol inside is the same by fixed national standards. You are buying the same grand Oxydol value, the same rich granulated soap.' In total war everyone did their bit.

On a much more serious note many other pieces of early of Second World War ephemera featuring Hitler are even more collectable. Broadsheets, printed with the text

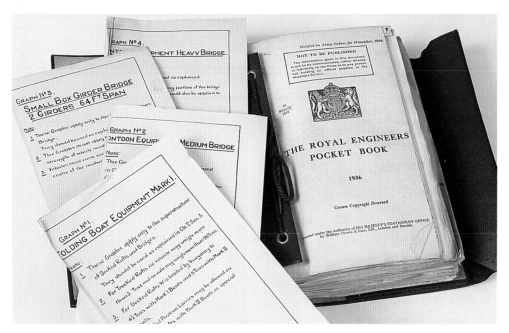

A complete *Royal Engineers Pocket Book* from 1936, as used by a soldier during WWII. It is still quite easy to find the individual component sections to such operational manuals. Updates were added as and when new developments occurred. However, finding a complete set, be they for engineers, infantry men or artillerymen, all bound in a leatherette cover and including original supplementary pull-outs as shown in this example, is becoming more difficult.

of Hitler's famous 'Last Appeal To Reason' speech, which drifted from the clouds over England in July 1940, are perhaps the rarest of all. Printed with the text of a speech the Führer delivered to the Reichstag on 19 July, where he implored the British people to rebel against the 'bourgeoisie' governing them, many of these quite fragile publications fell straight out of the bomb bays of Heinkels and Dorniers and straight into the hands or Britons, who promptly used them as lavatory paper. Preserving these communications was considered unpatriotic. Existing examples deserve to be saved.

It's difficult to appreciate today, but by the late 1930s civilians feared attack by airborne poison gas in precisely the same way that later generations feared the four-minute warning of a nuclear strike. Following the deadly use of chlorine, phosgene and lewisite (mustard gas) amidst the trenches of the Western Front during the First World War, most people assumed that it would be used again – this time delivered from the air by the new breed of high-speed mono plane bombers. Considered opinion held that the 'bomber would always get through', so an enormous amount of printed material supported the more tangible aspects of Air Raid Precautions, such as the ubiquitous gas masks and blast-protected taped windows. Leaflets advised people to always carry their gas masks, how to build a bomb-proof shelter (preferably under the stairs, which was considered the most robust place inside) and how to tape and seal gaps around doors

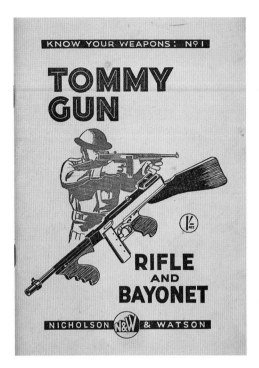

Even though British troops had encountered German sub-machine guns such as the Bergmann MG15 during WWI, until intelligence reports following the evacuation at Dunkirk revealed that many British soldiers were very impressed by the MP 38, or Maschinenpistole 38, weapons wielded by some German infantrymen, Britain's High Command generally discounted such weapons. The sudden fall of France in June 1940 meant that a shipment of Model 1928 Tommy guns destined for the French government was sent to Britain instead. Consequently, publisher Nicholson & Watson's guide to the weapon proved of enormous use to the members of the Home Guard and RN Commandos who were issued with the iconic machine gun.

Gale & Polden again, this time with an instructional handbook for a sub-machine gun, the STEN, which the British decided to manufacture. The name STEN is an acronym, combining the names of the weapon's chief designers, Shepherd and Turpin, and EN for Enfield (the Government's main ordnance factory). More than 4 million of these easy to produce weapons were manufactured, in of all places, the Tri-ang toy factory in Merton, Surrey. A huge quantity of STEN guns were dropped to the French resistance.

and windows to prevent the admission of poisonous gas. Most communications, especially the series of Civil Defence Public Information leaflets, were serious. Some, like the seaside postcards advising nudists to at least don a gas mask, were frivolous.

Many of these publications can still be found and provide the ideal supplement to a collection of larger objects like respirators, firstaid kits and decontamination outfits. Combined, these items tell the story of a harrowing period in Britain's island history.

The wartime emergency encouraged the publication of a wide range of useful handbooks. This one, *The Bren Light Machine Gun. Description, Use and Mechanism*, hails from the prolific stable of Aldershot's Gale & Polden. The Bren was a modified version of a Czechoslovak-designed light machine gun and was introduced into the British Army in 1935. The Bren's name was derived from Brno, the Czech city where the foreign weapon was originally designed, and Enfield, the site of the British Royal Small Arms Factory.

Three WWII Barnards pocket books. From left to right: *Manual of Rifles*, *Manual of Small Arms and Special Weapons* and *Manual of Modern Automatic Guns*. With so many men in the Home Guard and with virtually every boy in Britain following the deeds and actions of those on active service in the Army, there was a ready market for 'how to' guides about everything associated with military life. Barnards was one of the most prolific publishers of accessible tutorials about everything from the more familiar .303 Lee-Enfield, which was first introduced in 1895, to the more modern 9mm STEN gun, introduced in 1941.

One of a comprehensive series of publications produced by HMSO (His Majesty's Stationery Office) during WWII intended to keep people up to date with the progress of individual campaigns or service arms, *Coastal Command* is a good example of the kind of inexpensive collectable that's ideal to kick-start a collection. Produced by the million, these booklets are still pretty easy to find.

Although many women joined the ranks of the ATS, Women's Land Army, WAAF and ARP amongst numerous other National Service organizations in the Second World War, with most able-bodied men drafted into the forces, the majority of women stayed at home. The exigencies of total war imposed severe restrictions on the supply of imported goods and meant that much

Published in 1941, Penguin's *Warships at Work* was written by A.C. Hardy, who continued to write books about maritime matters after the war. Illustrator Laurence Dunn began life sketching fishing boats in Brixham Harbour, where he grew up. During WWII, his interest in ships got him a job at Admiralty Intelligence, where his abilities to accurately reproduce the profiles of ships proved a great aid to recognition. Post-war he worked for many different shipping lines and even worked for the legendary *Eagle* comic. Dunn died in 2006.

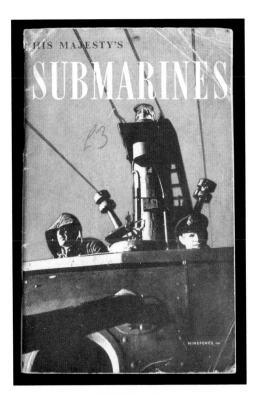

Another popular HMSO publication, *His Majesty's Submarines*, was published in 1945 and told the public as much as the authorities could about the 'silent service'. British films, such as 1943's *We Dive at Dawn*, and *Above Us the Waves*, which was made in 1955, filled in the gaps.

home-produced material was directed to the war effort. Rationing of food, fuel and clothing was the result. With great ingenuity cookery writers and chefs devised numerous recipes to help housewives eke out the meagre rations and make the most of a limited supply of ingredients. The numerous recipe books and handbooks advising the most economic use of ration coupons (there were even quiz booklets explaining the rules behind the ration amounts established for clothing, footwear, cloth and – important for 1940s' housewives – knitting yarn.

Combining a selection of the numerous publications from the so-called 'kitchen-front' with wartime editions of women's magazines and ration books builds an interesting and increasingly valuable collection.

Staying with the ladies, another popular area to collect relates to fashion. Women of all ages like to look good – an attitude that wartime restrictions did little to dent. Even if women couldn't buy the latest fashions as readily as before they could at least 'make do and mend'. They could also create things from scratch using linen perhaps put away 'for a rainy day' before hostilities began. Not surprisingly then, lots of 'sixpenny' patterns can still be found. These range from 'War-time Renovations', showing how old garments could be transformed into the latest cuts, to 'Economy Frocks', encouraging women to make modest dresses from the cheapest available fabrics. Collectors less inclined to opt for such 'girlie' material might at least consider 'New Woollies for our Sailors, Soldiers and Airmen', which at least featured pictures of fighting men on the cover – albeit in rather camp cardigans and Fair Isle sweaters.

Not strictly ephemeral, because they were certainly intended to last a long time, this chapter is probably the best place to discuss wartime souvenirs and 'trench art'. It's a truism of military service that a lot of time is spent simply waiting for something to happen. Many old soldiers remember wartime service as being long periods of tedium interspersed with sudden moments of terrifying activity. While waiting for the order to go 'over the top' or advance towards a distant objective on a map, amongst many other

Printed in 1945 in Germany, *30th Corps in Germany* is an eighty-page booklet full of photos and maps 'which tells who we are, where we are, why we're here and what happens next.' It was XXX Corps' failure to arrive at the Arnhem Bridge as planned that ultimately caused Operation Market Garden to fail. This book is an account of the duties and activities of Lieutenant General Brian Horrocks's famous formation when it came to the end of its journey and found itself at rest in a shattered Third Reich. It's pleasing to find an example of this relatively common publication with its maps in place.

With Britain only really vulnerable to attack from the air it was most crucial that everyone, civilian and serviceman alike, could spot enemy aircraft overhead. Aimed at the younger reader, *The ABC of Aeroplane Spotting* was published by Raphael Tuck & Sons, a family business established in Bishopsgate in the City of London in 1866. Initially known for their greetings cards, they became famous for selling postcards. Ironically given the subject matter of this book, Tuck's was all but destroyed by a Luftwaffe bomb in December 1940, but survived the war and became part of the giant BPC printing conglomerate in 1959.

distractions, soldiers of every generation whiled away the time reading, singing bawdy barrack-room ballads or writing home to loved ones.

As discussed earlier in this book, some of the most poignant relics of both world wars are the delightful embroidered postcards soldiers posted home. These delicate, often filigree missives, contrast dramatically with the tired, battledress-clad fighting men who penned them. It is equally moving to discover that lace-decorated cards with the message 'Souvenir of the BEF' were posted by young British soldiers stationed in France both in 1914 and 1940.

Collecting such sentimental relics also helps the military enthusiast gain a fuller picture of the soldiers' lives.

'Let Milk Be Your Health Warden'. Like most other things, milk was rationed during WWII. But it was important and its virtues were stressed. The weekly adult ration was three pints (1,800ml) but this occasionally dropped to just two pints (1,200ml) per adult per week.

US support was critical to enable Britain to remain in the war. Along with essential foodstuffs, oil, iron and steel, North America also provided war planes that could be pressed into front-line service. This guide provided a useful look at the types of American aircraft in service with both the RAF and Fleet Air Arm.

Although often heavily censored or containing the sparest details about the location or activities of the writer, what words there are often paint a more realistic picture of military service than countless biographies by distant commanders could ever archive. Examples of such communications, posted just before a seismic event, like the Battle of the Somme in 1916 or Dunkirk evacuation in 1940, also contribute to our contextual understanding of military history.

With such a vast amount of ordnance being lobbed to and fro across no-man's-land by opposing armies, it's hardly surprising that bored soldiers decided to fashion some of the thousands of spent shell cases in to battlefield souvenirs. Consequently, unwanted brass cases were fashioned into a wide range of containers, vases and, commonly, ashtrays. Generally these objects were decorated with often quite sophisticated etched designs revealing naïve messages such as 'Souvenir of the First World War' or 'Allies in Arms'.

Prisoners of war obviously had plenty of free time on their hands. Like their colleagues at the front line, POWs fashioned souvenirs from whatever materials they could lay their hands on. Whilst not of the sophistication perhaps of the ship models painstakingly fashioned from bone and ivory by Napoleonic prisoners, examples of the handiwork of

When They Sound the Last 'All-Clear' sheet music. One of 'Forces Sweetheart' Vera Lynn's most popular songs, first recorded in 1941 (music by Hugh Charles, lyrics by Lewis Elton), the reassuring all-clear was signified by a single siren note and meant the bombers had passed and things were back to normal. 'When they sound the last all-clear how happy, my darling, we'll be. When they turn up the lights and the dark lonely nights are only a memory.'

twentieth-century POWs are still enlightening. Italian prisoners, for example, having mostly demonstrated their willingness to comply with the rules of their captors and as a result being trusted to work on the land in Britain and fraternize peacefully with British civilians, had better access to materials needed to make toys and dolls. These craftworks were often exchanged for rations. Interestingly, the author recalls his mother telling him that when a child in war-torn central London, the best place to obtain sweets and fancies was from the prisoners in Italian POW cages!

Chapter 7

Detecting Fakes and Caring
for your Collection

The supply of authentic military collectables is naturally finite and with each passing year fewer genuine items come onto the market. As a consequence, the law of supply and demand naturally dictates that prices rise in direct relation to the availability of, or lack of, such original items. The same law also encourages the unscrupulous to pass off fakes as the real thing. But 'faking' in itself needs some clarification. Items sold to enthusiastic re-enactors and militaria buffs as reproduction, or 'repro', articles aren't fakes, they are honest replicas. These items belong as much to the world of costume hire as they do to historical regalia. Indeed, these days, dealers in real militaria collectables often supplement their income by trading in goods for hire. That perennial TV favourite *Dad's Army* has ensured that many a fancy dress party features a smattering of 'Captain Mainwarings' and 'Private Pikes'.

It's much harder to determine if something sold for a premium as being 'genuine Second World War' or 'as worn during the Battle of Britain' is real or not. Often we collectors are so keen to get our hands on that one object that will fill a gap in our collections that we actually want to believe the object of our desires is the genuine item. And this is where the first and most basic test for determining something's veracity should be applied: If it sounds too good to be true, it's probably a lie. Everyone knows that the real McCoy – be it a Third Reich tunic badge, nineteenth-century French impressionist painting or a piece of rare Delft art pottery cloisonné tile – will cost a lot of money. Now, whilst it is of course possible to unearth that 'once in a lifetime' find at a car boot sale or village fete it is almost never likely to happen when dealing with … a dealer. Most are a hundred per cent honest but some are unscrupulous and in it only for profit. Remember, you get nothing for nothing.

Another simple test, most suitable for badges and other metal items, is the 'weight test'. We have an innate ability to tell if something feels wrong because it is too light and tinny. But again, caution is required. Towards the end of the Second World War Nazi Germany employed a lot of very lightweight alloys for the production of badges and insignia. Steel and other heavy metals were used for tanks and U-boats. Similarly, novice collectors shouldn't think that silver plastic Scottish, Queen's Own Cameron Highlanders Glengarry badge was made in Hong Kong in the 1960s. As in Germany,

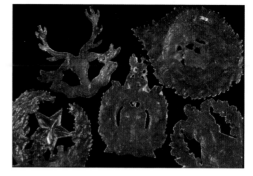

Badges that at first glance might appear to be fakes can turn out to be manufacturers' samples intended only for display. To facilitate ease of mounting within a display they were often produced with flattened or wax-filled backs. This assortment of Scottish badges includes those of the Argyll and Sutherland Highlanders, the King's Own Scottish Borderers, the Cameronians (Scottish Rifles) and the Seaforth Highlanders.

the exigencies of war meant that raw materials were in short supply in Britain (we all know about rationing) and long before the victories of 1945 plastic economy badges, black, brass-colour and even red for the emblem of a Ministry of Supply Salvage Steward, as well as the aforementioned silver, were introduced in place of heavier metals like brass. Obviously it is almost impossible to detect every attempt at subterfuge. In their efforts to deceive, dishonest sellers who possess the right tools can easily add a spurious date stamp to an item, suggesting it is older than it actually is. And steel helmets have long been subject to the addition of decals and painted insignia to make them more interesting and valuable.

My father spent many years as an infantryman in the British Army, retiring as an RSM. As a young man he was a keen badge collector. This is what he told me: 'Today, badge collectors have to be especially careful to avoid damaged or fake items. One way to avoid costly mistakes is to purchase items from reputable dealers. Many magazines, such as the Army's own periodical *Soldier*, feature advertisements from reliable merchants. One tip that can help avoid buying a "wrong'un" is to look at the reverse of a badge to see if the impression is clear, as it should be if officially struck. Collectors

Nazi German cloth and metal insignia are the most commonly faked. They can be easily aged. It's amazing what burying a 're-strike' in a watered pot plant for a week or two can achieve. And for eons tea has been the favoured choice of counterfeiters when they want to stain paper or cloth with the patina of age. Gone are the days when enthusiasts could rely on UV (or 'black') light to expose synthetic fibres. Polyester, lurking cuckoo-like in a badge purporting to be made of cotton or wool, revealed itself in all its man-made glory. Today, many fakes, not reproductions, are manufactured in the Far East, where natural fibres are still in daily use. So this classic test is not as useful as it was. Experience counts for everything and very quickly even the inexperienced will be able to tell gold from fool's gold.

The value of this WWII Durham Light Infantry (DLI) King's Crown economy Bakelite cap badge has been drastically reduced by damage to the lugs on its back. These are used to secure the badge to the cap by the addition of a spit brass pin and backing plate. This rare badge has been ruined by bad storage, perhaps by stacking badges on top of one another without sufficient protective packaging, causing the protruding lugs to fail. Collectors beware and check the lugs on the reverse of such badges before parting with hard-earned cash. If broken, the lugs are almost impossible to repair satisfactorily.

should also avoid badges where repair to the hasps or lugs is evident, or which have perfectly flat backs rather than the concave detail that results from a complex impression on the face of thin sheet metal. The front of the badge should obviously be clearly defined, with the regimental title clear and easy to read – although some leeway should be allowed for previous cleaning, of course (but there's little value in an item with much of its detail rubbed away by years of vigorous "bull").'

Another very experienced enthusiast and a dealer to boot, but a scrupulously honest one, is Sabre Sales' Nick Hall. Nick told me that faking military regalia isn't a new thing. 'After the Napoleonic Wars, there was a desire to commemorate and celebrate the regiments involved in the campaigns. The result was that there was actually a firm, also in Southsea, where Sabre is based, established to manufacture shako plates to sell to collectors, just as there was then a demand and fashion to manufacture two- dimensional, rather than three-dimensional, armour and cast-iron battleaxes to decorate gothic houses and flats. So there was a demand for such items long ago and with Britain being the world's premier manufacturing location, it made such repro items to meet the demand of collectors.' Nick also told me that the demands of active service meant that when a British regiment was serving overseas, for example, and the quartermaster's stores had run out of spare badges, 'the various bazaars' adjacent to the unit's posting would be sought as a supply for replacements. He said: 'If a British regiment was stationed in Egypt, for example, they couldn't ring up one of the major badge manufacturers back

 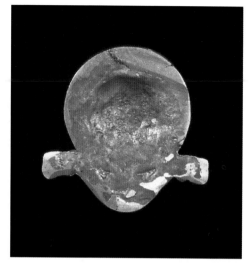

The front face of this Royal Scots Fusilier cap badge looks acceptable but once it is turned over a re-strike, or fake, is revealed. This badge has been produced by simply taking a mould, an impression, of a genuine badge, into a soft compound. When the badge is removed from the mould a suitable molten alloy is poured in and when cooled, the finished badge is removed. Naturally this process only manages to reproduce the front face. As this image reveals, the reverse is a lamentable failure.

home and say they wanted some new badges. Not at all. In fact they would take a badge down to the nearest bazaar where a tradesman would get some very fine quality sand. The badge would be dipped in the sand and a new one would be cast in the resulting impression – a "sand cast". Before the metal solidified in the sand two metal plugs or a bar were stuck into the back. The result was that some regiments would have actually worn bazaar-made badges, although they were not renowned for their longevity and quality finish. Actually, in the 1950s and '60s both India and Pakistan were two of the major sources of repro badges in the world.' Are these locally sourced badges real or fake? Either way, Nick told me that serious badge collectors 'wouldn't really brook' such low-grade reproductions but he was keen to point out that some of the traditional theories about what constitutes a real or fake badge can be easily disproved. He also told me that just because a newly purchased, but allegedly vintage, badge was sharp and crisp, displaying none of the effects of the sort of cleaning one would expect from a service item, it wasn't necessarily a reproduction item. Many of the badges that found their way into the hands of dealers were disposed of, un-issued, fresh from army stores and were never subjected to such maintenance. Indeed he recalled purchasing a large quantity of original Duke of Cornwall's Light Infantry badges from a pawnbroker in Aldershot. He told me that all of these badges had 'razor sharp' edges because they were all still in their original boxes.

Ironically, although the current library of reference material is a boon to collectors it has also enriched the counterfeiter too and provided very accurate reference – not only

Famous battle patch of the British 1st Airborne Division, as worn on Dennison jump smocks. It features Bellerophon astride Pegasus. One way to test for authenticity in cloth insignia is to tease out a strand of fabric and touch it with a lit match. Synthetics will shrink before the flame!

of what a badge looks like – but how to detect fakes. Sadly, these books can be used as guides to help the dishonest create realistic fakes. Google images have simply exacerbated the situation! Nevertheless, consulting the many published works available, in print or online, will not simply give you an indication of values of course; it will also let you look at photographs of the real thing. Notice how crisp genuine badges are (repro items are often second-generation castings – the original badge being used as the pattern from which a plaster or silicone mould is cast). As is the case with most things in life, photos, prints, oil paintings, etc., every time a duplicate is made, quality is reduced.

A badge's face isn't the only place to investigate to determine if the item is a re-strike. Often, the authenticity of an item is best judged by simply turning it over. The majority of badges are manufactured from sheet metals that have been pressed; punched-out by a mechanical process so that all the detail is embedded in relief. Badges reproduced by a limited run casting process will often have flat, rather than concave backs. This is because when the alloy or other molten material has been poured into the mould, its liquid surface dries flat.

A quick note here about the lugs, pins and fixtures of cap and collar badges. Original items reveal a continuation of surface finish and tone that a badge with a recently soldered pin can never suggest. Don't let anyone trick you into believing that an example of remedial work on a badge or other item of militaria was a 'field repair'. In their day badges and items of military equipment were low value utilitarian pieces – when they broke or went missing, if possible they were replaced from quartermasters' stores. Alternatively, a few coins handed to a trader in a market place close to a unit's depot would deliver a replacement badge in time to avoid the RSM's wrath regarding the original's loss.

Combat infantrymen certainly didn't waste time mending insignia, so if someone tries to sell you a badge with a blob of solder attached to one of the badge's attachments it has probably been done to deceive. Some things to look out for: Firstly a change in the surface finish on a metal item suggesting it is the marriage of two different pieces; evidence of solder, file marks and–worst of all – traces of adhesive. Unless they are fresh from dark storage, period cloth items should exhibit some evidence of colour fading. Items that have supposedly been worn in combat without any trace of stitch marks, holes or loose threads have clearly never been in battle. Lastly but of no less importance, be aware of traces of a synthetic thread like nylon in any British badge during or before the Second World War.

The dramatic advances in computer-aided technology, allowing cutting, milling and die-stamping tools to be linked to mould etching or casting machines, makes the problem of 're-strikes' even more significant than ever before.

A 1970s' officer's slip-on rank insignia (captain) from either 1st, 2nd or 3rd battalion, The Queen's Regiment. To be worn on the epaulettes of the famous 'woolly pully'.

Study the apparent effects of age and wear. Do the scratches conform to the position of the attachment or slung equipment that would have caused the wear in the first place? If something were allegedly battle-worn and a survivor of the muddy soils of Vimy Ridge, would the delicate fabric backing really have survived so well? How has a piece of khaki serge, stored unnoticed for ninety years, really survived the predatory attentions of moths?

Though fewer and far between than they were, many reputable militaria dealers offer guarantees of some kind, especially with the higher priced items of equipment like nineteenth-century helmets or Third Reich regalia. Similarly, most reputable auction houses will refund the price paid for an item if it can be shown that in reality it does not have the authenticity promised by the company's catalogue listing.

Many collectors are happy with copies. Enthusiast Roy Smith sees this as a new and somewhat disappointing trend that can only serve to dilute the quality of existing military insignia in circulation today: He told me: 'When I first started collecting there were no reproduction insignia and the uniforms we sought were not for wear but to be displayed. Possibly I'm out of touch, but today the emphasis seems to be on re-enactment and original badges seem to be of little consequence.' This lack of concern about authenticity has made it easier for reproductions to be passed off as originals and high production standards mean that it is often very hard to detect fakes. This situation is exacerbated by the huge amount of US insignia around – the vast majority of it possibly never even having been worn in theatre. GIs could readily purchase replacement unit badges in their battalion PX (Post Exchange) and many simply collected examples of neighbouring units or purchased a variety of badges to be sent home to friends and family. US soldiers were permitted to own as many badges as they wanted – unlike the British squaddies' paltry cloth insignia two!

Collectors should note that US cloth insignia made in the UK while Uncle Sam's troops were garrisoned in the UK during the Second World War is of a quite different finish from that of US manufacture. So, it's easy to spot wartime originals. The essential

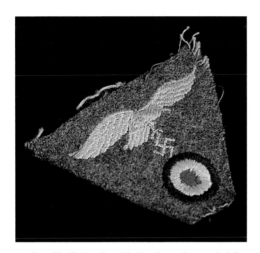

Luftwaffe Other Rank's Eagle and roundel for their distinctive M43 'ski cap' (as worn by Michael Caine in *The Eagle Has Landed*).

difference between patches of US or British manufacture is simple. American-made items are embroidered and those made under war economy conditions in the UK generally consist of overlaid pieces of stitched-together cloth. It's more difficult to identify those US officers' cap badges manufactured in the UK. Thousands were held in stock in US quartermaster stores in the UK theatre.

To be honest much American repro is almost impossible to detect. During and following the Second World War it was popular to collect US unit patches and sew them onto blankets. In America, dealers like 'The Patch King' made insignia to the same high standards as those destined for government issue. Generally, even today, British repro is not of such exacting standards and so is somewhat easier to detect. As time goes on, the current batch of re-enactor's uniforms are of a higher standard and perhaps in approximately twenty years' time will bear authentic wear and begin to appear 'of a certain age'. Certainly, there was a period when fake cloth insignia could be scanned with UV light to show man-made polyester fibre. But with the proliferation of material coming from the Far East – where much more natural fibres are still in daily use – detection is now more difficult. On the balance of probability, obscure pieces of uniform and insignia, appearing in isolation, are less likely to be fake. Provenance is everything. A battledress blouse or 'battle bowler', unearthed from granddad's attic and which can be attributed to a serving ancestor are doubtless genuine – the SS camo smock bought from a West End dealer perhaps less so.

Metal badges are not the only insignia subject to duplication. Fabric items are also reproduced, sometimes dishonestly. As with metal items, distinguishing real from fake cloth badges requires lots of experience. One of the ways enthusiasts can determine the authenticity of items is to smell them – the fibres of very old material have a distinctive 'musty' aroma. Although, the dishonest seller employs an armoury of techniques to age or distress an item, no amount of staining with weak tea can replace the smell of the genuine product!

There are some rather more elaborate methods to employ when trying to determine right from wrong as far as cloth insignia are concerned. One method is to attempt to tease out a strand of fabric from the edges of the badge (get the owner's permission though!). When touched by a lit match, man-made (synthetic) fibres will shrink, forming a round blob that retreats from the heat. On the other hand, cotton or woollen fibres, from which most pre 1950 badges were made, will simply burst into flames. Frustratingly, unless you can be sure cloth insignia has been removed from an obviously original uniform it can be very difficult to detect post-war fakes. The standards of manufacture are so high. Naturally, the same caution should be used when assessing the veracity of larger cloth items like uniforms. In the case of combat gear and greatcoats it is much more difficult to pass off fake items. No matter how well it has been conserved, 70 year-old serge has a pretty distinctive 'nose' that is almost impossible to replicate. But, you guessed it, things aren't that simple either. For example, Canada and France adopted Second World War battledress for their own troops- Canada as early as 1939, though their battledress uniforms were darker in colour with a distinctive green tinge to the dark khaki colour. The first French battledress was introduced in 1945 and was made of a heavy cotton duck but based on the same design as the British 1937 Pattern. In 1946 the French army introduced a woollen serge uniform that looked very similar to the British 1937 Pattern but with exposed buttons. It was used until the late 1950s. I know that for decades after the Second World War collectors bought Canadian, and sometimes French, battledress on the assumption that it was pucker British *schmutter*.

Simple Dishes For War-time was typical of the wide variety of books and pamphlets designed to help housewives make the best of the meagre rations available. Fortunately, because of the efforts of the newly formed War Agricultural Committees ('War Ags') Britain's farmers managed to double their yield during wartime, and despite the U-boat, which severely restricted imports of foodstuffs, the nation didn't starved.

With Waffen SS tunics selling for £1,000 plus, it makes commercial sense to commission a tailor to fabricate a copy of a 1940s, uniform item. In a sense, enthusiasts have shot themselves in the foot. Demanding ever more reference material, collectors of militaria and scale modellers have encouraged the growth of a massive publishing industry providing reference books detailing every conceivable uniform and regalia configuration displayed by the soldiers of virtually all the world's armies. So, there's plenty of authoritative source material for forgers to copy, ensuring that their reproductions are accurate enough to fool even the most knowledgeable. Conversely, although the current library of reference material has definitely enriched the hobby and enables collectors to see individual items in the context of their original purpose on campaign, these materials have also proved essential to the counterfeiter.

Not surprisingly perhaps given their popularity, by the mid-1990s stocks of German and even American Second World War military equipment were fast running out. While the repro industry geared itself to meet the needs of re-enactors and vehicle enthusiasts, British collectors began to select items of their native country's combat equipment. There was a surge in the collection of battledress blouses and trousers, enthusiasts being keen to configure a complete outfit and webbing still being plentiful.

There had been a huge influx of brand new battledress blouses in the 1980s when dealers took possession of the last surpluses that had languished in British Army stores since the National Service days of the 1950s. But by the 1990s most of this was exhausted. In fact, other than this supply, the only other stocks of surviving battledress on the market were officers' badged versions. Unlike soldiers and NCOs, officers owned their kit and were allowed to keep it when they left the colours. Although Commonwealth battledress could be found, British collectors didn't much fancy it. Apparently many re-enactors considered only the uniforms of Canadian, Australian and Indian troops related to the war in the Far East, despite of course these nations' gallant activities in Europe. One kind of battledress that was snapped up by British enthusiasts actually originated in Greece. Although it was of a slightly different finish to home-made uniforms and of course bore labels and stencilling bearing Greek script, for a long time it provided re-enactors with a perfect alternative to original uniforms.

Of the original wartime battledress that could be found, the most prized kind was the special pattern trousers worn by airborne troops. These possessed large 'bellows' front-leg pockets and two field dressing pockets at the rear. But even these presented problems because they were rarely in sizes suitable for the fuller figures of civilians who could eat what they wanted when they wanted and were not subjected to the regular exercise and calorie burn of soldiers in action. Most Second World War infantrymen invariably also had much narrower chests and slimmer waists than today's re-enactors.

There's another reason why so few authentic Second World War British uniforms survive: much of wartime Britain was put to the plough as the Women's Land Army toiled to cultivate every available inch of countryside. Civilians were encouraged to 'grow their own' and considerably expand their allotments. The advent of peace and the returning import trade reduced the need for so much arable land and the authorities feared that the parts of Britain where unprotected topsoil had been loosened and where hedgerows and trees had been removed to increase yield, might turn into dustbowls similar to those in the Midwest of the USA during the depression of the 1930s. With huge stocks of battledress surpluses one of the most obvious products of the peace dividend that came with demobilization was the decision to shred the majority of it and use it to bind the newly fallow soil.

It's worth mentioning here a bit about the added value given by association to uniforms displaying the traces, or 'shadowing', of previously applied insignia. 'Hang on, this jacket shows the outline of SS runes,' or perhaps 'this once featured an 82nd Airborne patch.' The added provenance given to a possibly mundane uniform if you can be sure of its history can add real value. Certainly, for collectors, jackets with their insignia intact are worth a premium price. Indeed, combined they are worth more than badges or battledress individually.

An awful lot of uniforms on the market have been 'doctored' by, perhaps, the addition of either real or reproduction insignia ... buyers beware. Many enthusiasts, though, seem happy and such 'combos' are still very collectable. One kind of uniform item hard to tamper with of course is the leather flying jacket. It's really not possible to disguise traces of needle holes in sheepskin or calf hide so few try to remove insignia and pass something off with spurious provenance but it is perfectly possible for emblems to be added to an otherwise nondescript item in an attempt to 'talk up' the value.

Purchasers of aeronautical items purporting to be of First World War vintage, such as RFC wrapover service

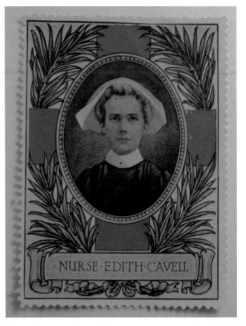

Portrait stamp issued to commemorate the death of nurse Cavell. A variety of other stamps and postcards about the incident were also published, many of them rabidly anti-German.

tunics (the characteristic 'maternity jacket') or the less iconic, but still rare, officers' khaki service tunic (RFC of army pattern) should beware. It's very difficult to guarantee the authenticity of such pieces. Many items were privately purchased and made by bespoke tailors and anyway, since Howard Hughes's *Hell's Angels* movie in the 1920s, many credible film costumes, manufactured using identical techniques as those used during wartime, have been absorbed into collections of genuine items.

Faked Second World War items are easier to detect. The sheer effort involved in weathering and aging reproduction Irvine flying jackets or Luftwaffe brown leather flight jackets is a major disincentive to fraudsters. Collectors should examine American flying jackets particularly closely. Many of the classic Second World War pilots' brown leather A-2 flying jackets have been enhanced with spurious painted insignia. Usually these colourful embellishments to the backs or breast panels of such jackets bear the unimaginative legends 'Pursuit Squadron' or 'Flying Tigers'. Painted decoration can be quite easy to distress to suggest age. Scuffs can be made with glasspaper and flexing can crack the surface finish; techniques that are often sufficient to suggest age.

It is possible to find examples of surviving authentic flying equipment and often what looks like the result of fraudulent meddling can be the genuine effect of long-term storage. For example, the author recently photographed a consignment of quite rare early pattern one-piece Sidcott Suits – the version with sheepskin collar and cuffs as

Evocative image of a WWII Women's Voluntary Service (WVS) helmet hanging, ready to use, on the stable door of a rural cottage. The WVS was established in 1938 as a support organization for ARP and its duties were set out in the 1938 Air Raid Precautions Act.

worn by RAF crews during the Battle of Britain. The suits had been folded and stored for perhaps fifty years. They were intact with a perfect cotton twill finish and superb sheepskin detailing, and their provenance could be assured by one tell-tale piece of evidence: After years in cold, sometimes damp storage, the teeth of the suit's zip fasteners had partially corroded, leaving a criss-cross pattern of faint rusty tracery etched into the fabric surface. Distressing of this kind is hard to fake.

This all allows me to neatly segue into an area that is perhaps most closely associated with aviation collectables than any other sector – battlefield archaeology. Today there's a thriving market in unearthing rusty battlefield relics so that such long-buried combat relics can be cleaned, sometimes restored to pristine condition and then put on display. Aircraft sometimes crash to the ground, particularly when they have lost a dogfight with an adversary or fallen foul of flak (ground anti-aircraft or AA fire) while damaged tanks and other battlefield vehicles are generally recovered for scrap or repair – ships, of course, sink out of reach to Davy Jones's Locker when destroyed. The entombed bits and pieces of planes generally remain undisturbed but within reach of anyone with a metal detector and a shovel. Britain is strewn with the remains of myriad RAF and Luftwaffe machines, many shot down during the Battle of Britain in 1940. Therefore the fields and hillsides of the Home Counties have long presented a happy hunting ground for enthusiasts determined to uncover the remains of a .303 Browning machine gun, a telescopic oleo leg from a Hawker Hurricane's undercarriage or Revi 16D gunfight off a Luftwaffe Ju88 night fighter. We've long been used to seeing twisted aluminium remains purporting to be part of the fuselage or control panel of a Second World War warplane but today it seems that even corroded army buttons and cap badges have a monetary value far beyond their apparent worth. As with all collectables, provenance is all-important, so if an artefact can be proven to have been located on the site of a First or Second World War battlefield its value will increase accordingly.

Probably the only area of military collectable of particular interest to the re-enactor and which by necessity depends upon the integration of certain non-original components

A selection of British and Prussian badges from WWI. The Royal Naval Air Squadron (RNAS) Armoured Car Section comprised squadrons of Rolls-Royce Armoured Cars and were used to protect the Royal Navy's aviation assets.

as spares or replacements, is the field of classic military vehicles. A functioning period military vehicle or aircraft will always be a compromise. A fusion of original and modern replacement parts combined during hours of painstaking restoration is really the only way enthusiasts can keep authentic US M3 half-tracks, British Daimler 'Dingo' scout cars, and German *Kubelwagens* on the road.

There is one last area from where reproduction items sometimes migrate into the hands of unwitting collectors. That sector in question? The property of props departments – the province of the studio departments manufacturing badges, regalia and uniforms used in TV programmes or in feature films. Sometimes, however, these 'repro' items can be worth even more than authentic wartime originals. If provenance exists that authenticates an item's role in a classic war film such as *The Bridge over the River Kwai, Lawrence of Arabia, A Bridge Too Far* or *Saving Private Ryan*, it can command top dollar. If it can be proved to have a direct association with one of the film's stars, its value will soar even higher.

With each year rare things become rarer and whilst the passage of time means that authentic military collectables from the twentieth century's two world wars and even more recent conflicts like the Vietnam and Falklands wars are getting to harder to find, in one sense, contemporary collectors have a real advantage. The Internet has brought virtually every available collectable into an enthusiast's home. Previous generations of militaria collectors had to post a cheque or postal order to a far-flung supplier and after a week or two would receive a closely-typed inventory that listed what badges or other items of military collectable were held in stock. Rarely were any photos or drawings attached to such price lists. Collectors bought on trust. Often when a selection was made, the item had gone out of stock, having been purchased by a rival fan who was that bit quicker off the mark. When the item did arrive it often bore no resemblance to the description offered on the catalogue sheet. Now, collectors can see colour photos of their object of desire and either buy off a dealer for a fixed price or win something for a bargain price on eBay if the particular auction doesn't attract too many rival bids. It's never been easier for the novice or experienced collector alike. Although there is less material available it is all concentrated in specific places and it is available from all over the world. If you are prepared to pay the price, even the scarcest or most obscure things can be obtained. The Internet isn't just great as a market place – it's also a fabulously comprehensive encyclopaedia, a unique resource where virtually everything can be discovered. YouTube enables enthusiasts and collectors to watch videos of like-minded aficionados explaining the specific differences between one type of kit – the British Enfield MKIII or MkIV rifle, for example (deactivated of course), or even enjoy a personal tour of a far-flung military museum.

I can't stress enough the need for enthusiasts and especially novice collectors to scrutinize genuine items in order to see exactly how the real thing is supposed to look. Books are a great place to start, but really a museum is the best place for the average collector to see the real thing. Therefore, I urge collectors to take pen and notebook to their nearest regimental museum. Ideally (if you live in Britain), I would recommend a pilgrimage to one of the following: National Army Museum (London), RAF Museum (London & Cosford), Imperial War Museum (London, Manchester and Duxford), Royal Navy Museum (Portsmouth) or the Fleet Air Arm Museum (Yeovilton). A visit to the Land Warfare Hall at IWM Duxford provides a brilliant opportunity for enthusiasts to see military uniforms from the First World War to the present day displayed on superbly animated mannequins positioned in imaginative dioramas that feature every kind of terrain and a selection of very rare military vehicles and tanks.

Whether your collection is small and on the threshold or greatness of already well-established, you want to be sure that the time and money invested isn't wasted because of damage to your items caused by poor storage or display.

Army badges, like the soldiers who wore them, might be quite tough but they are not indestructible. Whether they are of metal manufacture of made from fabric, there are certain things that can be done to prevent further deterioration. The late Hugh King's and Arthur Kipling's monumental 1970s' two-volume work *Head-Dress Badges of the British Army (1800-1979)* remains the bible for collectors of military cap badges but the authors didn't just concern themselves with identifying badges; they considered how to display collections as well. They advised collectors not to bother to arrange items for any kind of exhibition at home or to colleagues within a collectors' society, for example, until they were sure that the arrangement was comprehensive. You will waste a lot of time, they said, creating a lot of unnecessary additional work dismantling badges and then being forced to laboriously rearrange them for display.

Kipling and King encouraged even beginners to organize their finds and recommended arranging badges on white card (or material of another colour if it better suited the badges selected) and making holes through which the mounting pins and lugs could be inserted and secured on the reverse with sticky tape or thread. These doyens of the badge-collecting fraternity recommended interleaving said sheets with corrugated cardboard to prevent damage to badges. They also stressed how important it is not to have too many layers. The weight of hundreds of metal badges is not inconsiderable. Too many will only result in the pins and securing logs on the badges at the bottom of the pile bending, or even worse – snapping off all together. You might think that items like army badges designed for military service would be robust enough to survive most situations. But remember, when in service they were worn on headdress and uniform tunics, not packed away en mass in darkness without any free air circulation. Damp and humidity are big enemies to both cloth and metal. Fabrics will develop mould if they get wet and aren't thoroughly dried. Metal will corrode – remember 'rust never sleeps'. If, for whatever reason, items of regalia in your possession do get damp – perhaps they got wet during a rain shower at the militaria fair from whence you purchased them or maybe they have been stored in a damp cellar or shed – the first course of action is to make sure they are immediately and thoroughly dried. First off, carefully unpack each item and lay them out on a clean absorbent surface such as sheets of kitchen towel. Incidentally, if they are wrapped in tissue

NFS 'sweetheart' brooch. The National Fire Brigade came into existence in 1941 when the volunteer national Auxiliary Fire Service (AFS) was amalgamated with the myriad local authority brigades to create one, unified and coordinated national fire service.

and this is damp, discard it. After some of the moisture has been absorbed, carefully lift them off of the kitchen towel, turn them over and place them the other way up on new towels, discarding the previous sheets. This method can be employed for both metal and fabric insignia. Allow the items plenty of time to dry naturally and make sure they are in a location where there is free circulation of air. When all the badges are perfectly dry, it is time to carefully inspect them for damage. I use a toothbrush to carefully remove any debris and corrosion. Obviously, if too much deterioration has occurred, the value of the badge will be greatly compromised – it might even not be worth keeping. With fabric items it is possible to lift foreign matter from the surface of badges that might have developed a slight 'bloom' of mould by simply wrapping sticky tape – adhesive side outermost – around your finger and gently picking up any flecks of debris of the emblems surface. Staining is more difficult to remove. In general it is inadvisable to attempt any drastic remedial action but sometimes the marking is so severe, an item is unfit for display or as an addition to a collection unless it is cleaned. In extreme cases I have actually used proprietary stain remover, of the kind that comes in spray dispensers and is intended for application on garments before they are put into a washing machine, and carefully applied this (again with a soft toothbrush) to discoloured areas. Then, the affected portion is carefully rinsed in warm water and the drying process resumed again. This is strictly a last resort, but it can be successful and

I have removed ink stains and discolouration caused by damp packaging coming into contact with the fabric of an item of insignia. So it's worth trying.

Obviously, prevention is better than cure and avoiding moisture damage from happening in the first place should be a priority of the collector. Even if you have to resort to storing badges in boxes and consigning them to cupboards or more remote storage, if they are packed with forethought, there won't be a problem. Valuable collectable items should be carefully packed. Individual badges should ideally be wrapped in acid-free tissue paper and then separated from neighbouring pieces by layers of bubble wrap or quantities of expanded polystyrene chips. The addition of sachets of desiccated silica gel – the kind that come with new cameras – will absorb any moisture that might penetrate the box. Boxes that might conceivably get wet should be covered in plastic – be careful though that any moisture runs away from the box and that they aren't left sitting in pools of moisture that might have congregated, or worse, been directed, by the plastic applied to protect the contents! One of my most useful tips for storing things so that they will not suffer from the debilitating action of moisture sounds obvious but is often overlooked: Don't transfer items from one extreme of temperature to another. For example, in winter loft spaces can be quite cold – especially if the spaces between joists have been properly insulated. Boxes sitting atop these will be of a much lower temperature than the rooms inside the house. If these boxes are opened in a warm centrally-heated house and their contents of metal badges examined, but then repacked in the warm and then immediately replaced into the chilly loft, condensation may develop on the surface metal as it cools rapidly. Of course this can happen in reverse: Really cold items will feel quite damp if they are hastily unwrapped in a much warmer environment. All this activity will encourage corrosion.

Being derived from a natural source, latex (a milky substance found in some plants) rubber is not as durable as some entirely synthetic products like nylon and polystyrene. Even if subjected to vulcanization – the process invented by Charles Goodyear in 1839 and which improves its resistance and elasticity – rubber will perish. Modern processes reduce the risk but when one considers other materials used in the manufacture of gas masks, goggles, anti-gas capes and other rubberized cotton garments during the Second World War and before, rubber's unique molecular construction (something to do with proteins being broken down and oxygen molecules attacking the material's molecular double-bond structure!) vintage items are prone to turning brittle and cracking, going sticky or even decomposing. One way to avoid such irreparable damage to your prized items is to ensure that rubber artefacts are stored at a constant temperature which is neither too hot nor too cold. To prevent objects sticking to each other, such as a neatly folded gas cape for example, it is also worthwhile covering rubber items with a dusting of talcum powder. Rubber shouldn't be stored under compression either so piling up several weighty objects one upon another is not a good idea. For-long term preservation, gas masks are better removed from their original bags, boxes or tins and put away opened out. I have found it better to use bubble wrap of sheets of thin, flexible expanded polystyrene as interleaving, rather than acid-free tissue. After unpacking a respirator or pair of rubber-edged Luftwaffe goggles, to my horror I have discovered that acid-free tissue paper can stick to the viscous surface of slowly perishing rubber. Some collectors suggest the application of silicone in the form of furniture polish to reduce the stickiness of vintage rubber. Just how this might react with the aforementioned molecular structure of the material in the long term remains to be seen. Like rubber, leather is a natural product and like rubber it can be subject to deterioration if not properly treated. A variety of products can be used to feed and condition leather, the most well-known being saddle soap, and if the material is kept clean and stored at a constant temperature (ideally somewhere between 68°F and 77°F degrees Fahrenheit, out of direct sunlight and in neither a humid nor too dry environment), collectors should experience no problems with leather belts, gaiters, footwear or larger items such as sleeveless Second World War British Army leather battle jerkins.

Wartime 'Roll Out the Barrel' beer mug. Also known as the 'Beer Barrel Polka', this was an enormously popular song during WWII. The music was composed by the Czech musician Jaromír Vejvoda in the 1920s. It's possible that the song's success was partly due to the fact that the invasion of Czechoslovakia by Nazi Germany, and the subsequent worldwide emigration of thousands of Czechs to other parts of the world, caused this catchy tune to spread like wildfire.

Metal items have one main enemy – rust. Leather belts and equipment harnesses utilize numerous fittings to enable the suspension of a soldier's equipment. British Army webbing was littered with metal components, which present unique problems (as they did for their original owners) when trying to clean the brass buckles and fittings that made it all work. 'Button sticks' used primarily, as the name suggests, to clean brass buttons without getting Brasso polish on the fabric of uniforms, were also used to keep webbing from being plastered with the cleaner. As every National Serviceman will know, alongside Brasso, soldiers employed another famous brand – Blanco – to help maintain the meshed cotton material adopted as a replacement for leather after the Boer War. I would recommend collectors adopt precisely the same procedures to clean and service leather and webbing items employed by successive generations of soldiers.

A quick word about avoiding the use of cheap, metal coat hangers, especially when storing tunics and uniforms for a long time in an environment such as a garage the might be subject to dramatic changes in temperature and air movement. Being cheap these hangers are just good enough to transport garments on the short journey from the dry cleaners to home – but not much good for anything else. That's why they are cheap and that's why they can rust, leaving unsightly marks on vintage fabrics. It is much better to use plastic or wood hangers if at all possible.

I have found the best way to clean badges and intricate metal objects that are put on display and subject to dust is to use an 'air cleaner' of the type marketed to photographers. It is designed to blow dust from lenses and remove specks from inside camera backs or from digital sensors. They also make it easy to remove dust from the intricate recesses of badges. More stubborn debris can be removed by the more vigorous actions of a paintbrush.

Returning to storage – and assuming that although your collection is not on display and you don't want to consign your prizes to inaccessible storage in sealed boxes – I have found an extremely practical method of keeping dozens of badges safe, clean and close by. I use those metal multi-drawer cabinets sold by stationery shops and business equipment suppliers. These are intended to keep sheets of A4 documents neatly to hand. Although the march of the PC and the development of email and the Internet has greatly reduced the need to physically store sheets of typescript, these useful pieces of furniture are still manufactured. I have also found that by cutting a rectangle of foam around 1cm thick and placing it in the bottom of each draw covered by black velvet or a similar material, my badges can be safely stored ready for immediate inspection. The other advantage with these rather utilitarian items is that they don't look like the kind of place in which one might store valuables.

Now a word about the kind of natural discolouration of metal items like brass and deterioration of bronzed badges. Both brass and bronze are alloys of copper (two or more metals have to be combined to create an alloy). Gunmetal, bell metal and nickel silver are also copper alloys. Brass is an alloy containing about seventy per cent copper and thirty per cent zinc. Bronze has a much higher copper content, about ninety per cent, with six per cent tin and four per cent zinc. It is perfectly natural for uncoated copper alloys to develop brownish or even blackish tarnishes. These are the result of non-corrosive oxidization of the copper and are nothing to worry about. On many historic items like old army badges this patina testifies to the age of an object and is coveted by collectors. Sometimes this tarnish can accumulate quite thickly but this is nothing to worry about. On the contrary, it has the effect of preserving the base metal. Generally, it is not a good idea to use abrasive cleaners to polish the badge to a shine. Serving soldiers were ordered to do so. 'Bulling' badges was mandatory and woe betide any soldier who turned up on the parade ground with tarnished badges. Of course every time a soldier polished a badge or other brass accoutrement such as belt buckles or webbing attachments, he removed a quantity of metal. Similarly, every time a collector polishes a vintage badge he or she will be removing an amount of important surface detail. However, if amounts of bright-green powder are seen to accumulate on a badge's surface – especially in cavities – this is an indication of active corrosion, often known as 'bronze disease' or metal fatigue. This is to be avoided because if it is left unchecked it will result in pitting and the loss of surface detail. This form of corrosion is caused by the presence of salts in the air or left on the badge because of inappropriate cleaning, especially in humid conditions (I refer the reader to my earlier comments about maintaining constant humidity if possible). Dust and areas of surface dirt can actually trap moisture and encourage corrosion so it is important to ensure that cavities, especially, are carefully brushed clean.

A 3rd pattern parachutist helmet with webbing chinstrap of 1943 issue. The example shown belongs to either a Royal Signals paratrooper attached to airborne forces or perhaps a signaller who was part of a battalion of glider-borne troops. Amazingly, this helmet remained in service until replaced by the current Kevlar version in 1982. The helmet was once stored in a rural location and rodents nibbled its leather sweatband. Next to the helmet is a surviving British WWII parachute harness quick-release fitting.

Mishandling can also cause significant damage to metal badges. Many vintage army cap badges feature fine details that are easily bent or broken – I refer back to the Buffs cap badge mentioned in a previous chapter. Its tail, legs and feet are particularly susceptible to damage caused by rough handling. Even gentle handling with bare hands can cause problems. Our skin is rich with oils and the kind of salt deposits that are capable of corrosive action on alloys, especially brass. Fingerprints can actually etch themselves into the surface of an old badge, so it's wise to wear linen gloves of the sort that can be purchased in specialist photographic dealers when handling particularly valuable badges.

If a collector is forced to resort to cleaning a badge – perhaps it has been kept in a box full of old and dirty objects – then it is possible to do so with some quite simple materials. And yes, one of them is water, but because it will be applied and removed in a controlled and supervised manner its presence is nothing to worry about! Most conservationists recommend using a dilute solution of plain soap, about three per cent mixed with distilled water. If the badge has traces of grease or paint on it, prior to washing in the soap/distilled water solution, it is permissible to use a mineral spirit to gently wipe off such marks. It is even possible to use a ten per cent solution of proprietary cleaners such as Calgon to remove calcareous (lime or hard water) deposits that may have found their way onto a badge's surface. After all these treatments have been used, the item being cleaned should be given a final rinse in distilled water. To finish, the badges should be dried using kitchen towels, and once all traces of moisture has been removed, given a final inspection before storing, ideally in a container that includes some silica gel to absorb any traces of moisture invisible to the eye. I must stress that cleaning a badge should only be attempted if the item is in really poor shape and encrusted with grease, dirt or paint. In general it is far wiser to leave a badge alone and in its original condition.

Humidity can be a problem for displayed, as well as stored items. Badges exhibited behind glass in collectors' cabinets can suffer from the dramatic changes in temperature within our modern, centrally heated homes. Be careful that cloth insignia displayed in such a way does not come into contact with the glass front of the cabinet. This material can transfer heat by convection and affect the condition of any material with which it is in contact. Ideally it is a good idea to permit some air flow around displayed objects and it is important to ensure that moths and other predators can't get inside a cabinet.

Light is another important consideration. Direct sunlight will fade both uniforms and cloth badges – especially those where red or scarlet dominate within the design. As every artist knows, red is the most fugitive pigment. This is why red oil paint that will last is expensive and why red cars look good when brand new but rather decrepit within only a few years. Sunlight not only fades but is a source of heat. You would be amazed at how quickly the small space inside a display cabinet can heat up if it is subjected to sunlight. In the same vein, it is also important to avoid displaying items, especially those made from dyed fabric, in a cabinet with internal lights. The atmosphere inside will soon become very warm indeed and, when the illumination is switched off late at night, the aforementioned cycle of temperature extremes and humidity will begin all over again.

Another seemingly obvious thing to think about before you prepare items for display is to ensure they can be easily removed or at least be dusted. Unless you install your prizes into a hermetically sealed glass-fronted container, even the best display cabinet will admit an amount of household dust. It is unavoidable, especially if you use a cabinet of the most typical sort where the entire front is hinged to open and shut. On the other hand, some of the purpose-built cabinets manufactured for badge collectors do tend to suggest that their contents might be worth stealing. As we read earlier, thieves tend to like pinching badges but despite the fact that some of the more elaborate display cases manufactured are best avoided unless you have an elaborate security system or a pair of Rotweillers at home, some other items on the market are very worthwhile indeed. There are lots of very handsome compartmented display cases available. Manufactured from leatherette-covered chipboard or MDF and fitted with flock-covered trays or velvet liners, these units can be the perfect solution. Those with deeper pockets can opt for versions manufactured in solid oak or perhaps finished in a walnut or rosewood veneer! Often intended for wall hanging, these devices are equally suitable for placing in a drawer or on top of a shelf. Some quality display cases are manufactured in the form of shallow trays, which are often pressed from a single piece of metal to ensure stability. Into these flock-covered, compartmentalized vacuum-formed inserts can be placed badges of varying dimensions to be safely stored. Often, display cases of this type feature glazed fronts that can be opened and secured with side struts, allowing the enthusiast to rearrange the case's contents. A much cheaper, but no less practical method of display and storage is simply to use an artist's display folio. Many of these come with ready fitted transparent plastic pockets and are available in a variety of sizes from A4 to the massive A0 format. These pages can be used to display a wide range of items. It is especially easy to put cloth badges into such cases, but even metal insignia can be displayed in them. Individual badges simply have to be put inside separate plastic pouches and then two or three of these can be affixed inside one A4 pocket, for example. Of course a number of metal badges will reduce the available display space – especially when the required foam interleaving has been placed between pockets to avoid damage caused by metal pressing against metal.

Chapter 8

Making the Most of Your Hobby

Collecting is a disease that once contracted is very hard to cure. Fortunately, unlike most other ailments, it is quite harmless and won't damage your health. But beware; it might do serious damage to your finances.

Seriously, whilst some collections can get out of control and consume a disproportionate amount of ready cash, time and focus and result in the enthusiast spending hours engaged in solitary pursuit, most collections expand to plan. Organized collections grow steadily as aficionados discover that one route of investigation leads to another, then another – and very soon reveal myriad paths of undiscovered opportunity. What might start with a desire to collect only British RN Commando insignia, for example, can soon develop into a search for international insignia belonging to the Special Forces of foreign combatants.

But then that's the real fun of collecting. Often derided as solitary and myopic, and as covetous as Tolkien's famous Gollum, who was corrupted by the one true Ring, which he loved yet really desired to be free of, true collectors aren't just on a quest for financial investment or to hoard riches. Instead, they realize that their hobby is a great way to learn and discover; for enthusiasts history is made truly tangible. Most collectors also realize that they are, in a small but important way, helping to preserve a diminishing heritage.

Just because you are a collector doesn't mean you are a nerd. Indeed, you might be surprised to discover that many celebrities have caught the collecting bug. Hollywood superstars naturally have the time and money required to amass interesting collections. For example, Nicolas Cage is a long-time collector of both rare and vintage comic books and European sports cars, Dan Aykroyd collects police badges and, allegedly, Johnny Depp accumulates insects and rare books. Quentin Tarantino likes board games and Ben Stiller is a devoted 'Trekkie', once telling the TV audience of a *Star Trek* commemorative: 'I have two pairs of ears from the original series, both signed by Leonard Nimoy!' A little closer to the subject of this book, John Travolta has built up a unique collection of aviation memorabilia. Oh, and he's also a certified private pilot and owns five aircraft, including a Boeing airliner! Ex-Genesis band member and now solo superstar, Phil Collins is one of the foremost experts on the Battle of the Alamo and in 2012 published a book about his collecting habit. *The Alamo and Beyond: A Collector's Journey* explains how Mr Collins became hooked on the story after seeing the Disney

Major Donaldson's wartime activities with Intelligence Corps (I Corps) are still largely a mystery to his son Peter, the well-known BBC Radio 4 announcer and newsreader. 'He had languages and I think he was one of the very last British soldiers out of Crete,' he told me. Donaldson Senior had arrived there following the British Army's shambolic departure from mainland Greece in April 1941, where he had previously been stationed in Athens.

Peter does know, however, that his father's facility with languages was put to good use in North Africa, his next stop following his arrival in Alexandria. While based in Egypt Major Donaldson interrogated captured German Afrika Korps prisoners.

Major Donaldson's twin sons were born in Cairo in 1945. He left the Army in 1948 and moved again, this time to Cyprus in 1952, at the time of the military coup d'état that deposed King Farouk.

Peter told me that his father 'worked for the German Embassy in Nicosia for many a year, translating papers from Greek to German and from English to German.'

In 1984, in recognition of these services to their embassy, the Bundesrepublik Deutschland awarded Robert Donaldson the Verdienstkreuz am Bande, the Order of Merit of the Federal Republic of Germany, the only federal decoration of Germany that has been created by the nation's first president, Theodor Heuss, in 1951.

Before he could wear the German order, a striking golden commander's cross, enamelled in red with a central disc bearing a black Eagle suspended from a red ribbon with gold-black-gold stripes, retired British Army officer Donaldson had to apply to Buckingham Palace to wear it. On 21 August 1984, the British High Commission at Alexander Pallis Street, Nicosia invited the elderly recipient to 'call in at this office at your convenience'. The consular first secretary wanted to pass a document to Donaldson. And what a document! Neatly typed on Buckingham Place notepaper were the words: "I have the honour to inform you that The Queen has been graciously pleased to grant to you unrestricted permission to wear the insignia of the Government of the Federal Republic of Germany in recognition of your services."

After protocol had been observed Donaldson was free to accept the award from the German Ambassador, to whom he wrote: 'I feel very privileged and should like to ask you, dear Mr Ambassador, to convey my sincere thanks for this award to the Federal Government in Bonn.'

series *Davy Crockett, King of the Wild Frontier* in the 1960s. He recalled: 'When I was five or six I started dressing up like Davy Crockett.' While on tour with Genesis in the 1980s he discovered an original Davy Crockett letter in a shop in Washington DC and the die was cast. Collins's collection is allegedly kept in the basement of his house in Switzerland and includes Davy Crockett's musket-ball pouch (complete with five musket balls) and a knife belonging to Jim Bowie, no less.

So, as you can see, the novice collector is in good company.

In 1947 this very interesting badge was presented to Major Robert Donaldson by Dowodztwo Jednostek Wojsk Na Srodkowym Wschodzie, the Polish High Command of Military Units in the Middle East. At that time Major Donaldson was an officer in I Corps and based in Egypt.

After their nation's defeat in 1939, the Polish government in exile quickly organized an army of 75,000 men who had fled occupation. Initially based in France, these soldiers were involved in the Norwegian Campaign and the defence of France. Many Polish soldiers ended up in the French mandate of Syria, forming Rifle Brigade Carpathian under the leadership of General Stanislaw Kopanski. Nearly 20,000 Polish fighting men made it to Britain, around 5,000 of them aircrew. Those Poles who fell into Soviet occupation when Poland was divided between Stalin and Hitler in 1939 were subsequently released and evacuated to Persia under the Sikorski-Mayski Agreement in July 1941, which followed the Nazi invasion of the USSR and the Soviet's sudden change of sides. In the Middle East these newly liberated soldiers joined with those already in Syria. Initially led by General Wladyslaw Anders, by 1943 they had become known as the Second Polish Corps, under overall British control and that of General Sikorski, the exiled Polish leader in England. In August and September 1943, Second Polish Corps was moved to Syria and Palestine, and then to Egypt, and began preparing to be sent to the Italian front. On 7 May 1944, Poland's army in the east was renamed Military Command Units in the Middle East, headed by former Deputy Commander of the Army General Michael Tokarzewski-Karaszewicz. Polish muscle provided an important supplement to Allied forces and in the years 1944–1945, the Polish armed forces fought in Italy, France, Holland, Belgium and Germany. Despite performing their duty in Occupied Germany and Italy in the years following 1945, Polish forces who had served under Allied command were unceremoniously disarmed and their units disbanded by the British in 1947. The Polish Resettlement Corps (PRC) was created for those soldiers who did not want to return to a Stalinist Poland and about ninety per cent of Second Corps remained in exile. The PRC was disbanded after fulfilling its purpose in 1949.

Keen-eyed readers will notice the Islamic motif, details representing Middle Eastern vegetation and architecture as well as the distinctive Piast Eagle, emblem of the first ruling Poland. Until 1989, when the nation finally freed itself from Soviet bloc control, this heraldic embellishment would disappear from Polish insignia. The accompanying Polish certificate granted Major Donaldson the right to wear the insignia.

Most of us, of course, don't have the resources of Hollywood A-listers or pop stars who not only have wallets thick enough to satisfy their desires but also enjoy the support of personal assistants who help them source items they might fancy. But on the other hand, collectors like John Travolta and Phil Collins don't enjoy the freedom to pop in, unnoticed, to museums or attend car boot sales or collectors' jumbles like most of us do. So, in many ways the playing field is more even.

As I have mentioned before in this book, when I was a youngster the opportunities to easily build my collection were really quite limited. There were of course the posh antiques shops in select districts of major cities but these were way beyond my reach. 'Back in the day', tyros like me had to contend with 'junk shops' (since renamed 'collectors' centres'), the occasional antiques fair in the local church hall and the vagaries of ordering something from a series of Xeroxed sheets featuring columns of closely spaced typewritten copy. These lists didn't feature photographs; techniques we take for granted today weren't available until the late 1970s.

Interesting photo taken in the early 1990s of a WWII communal bomb shelter that survived – and I hope it still does – in Steyning, Sussex. You can just see the outline of the main entrance which was sealed after the war. Quickly constructed from ordinary house bricks, these surface shelters were capped with concrete slab roofs, which many thought insubstantial. However, they provided useful refuge for those caught out in the open during a raid or for citizens who lived in flats and didn't have access to an Anderson shelter in the garden. Inside were rows of wooden bunk beds, some four beds in height.

So, everything worked on trust. You trusted that your initial request for the list saw your addressed and stamped envelope returned. When you wrote again (calling was generally not an option as those trading in items such as military collectables usually had a day job and their 'business activity' was generally a sideline), you waited patiently for at least twenty-eight days before you opened the Jiffy envelope that had been despatched to you to check that you received what you had ordered.

Today those starting out in the hobby have no idea of how fortunate they are and experienced collectors like myself can't avoid comparing the ease of organising a collection with the pain and hassle involved in yesteryears. Fittingly, we have a Brit, Sir Tim Berners-Lee, the inventor of the World Wide Web, to thank for this massive leap. He proposed the basic system of data transfer between individual PCs and servers connected to the Internet in 1989. But, me being a fair-minded person and this being a tome aimed at fans of all thing military, we must not forget that the whole caboodle owes a lot to the North America's Advanced Research Projects Agency Network (ARPANET), which was part funded by the US military as a way of constructing a communications network that might survive the massive electromagnetic pulses generated by a nuclear attack. Thanks to packet switching and the development of transmission control protocols on the Internet (TCP/IP), we can now search dealers' collections, check out colour photos and even videos or items we wish to purchase online and from the comfort

A fascinating WWII Civil Defence relic that survives to this day in Lord North Street, Westminster, one of the finest Georgian streets in London. The words 'Public Shelter in Vaults Under Pavement in this Street' are presumably all that remain from the time of the Blitz, the cellars now appearing to have been converted into residential dwellings.

of our own homes. The Internet has put a world of collectables at our fingertips.

The exponential development of the web hasn't just put collectors into direct and efficient contact with shops and dealers, of course; it has also made researching your chosen topic that much easier as well. Armed with information gleaned from online directories even the most inexperienced collector will have a much better understanding than ever before of their chosen field or of the construction and appearance of a specific item. The rapid development of social media and video-sharing resources like YouTube means that it's even possible to see live action demonstrations of items so that the novice can get a better idea of not only the psychical appearance of a particular item but its contextual use. We can now see re-enactors slowly put on a set of British 1937 pattern webbing to get a better understanding of how Bren pouches are suspended or bayonet frogs fit to belts. In 1597 Sir Francis Bacon wrote 'knowledge is power' and it is as true today. The World Wide Web has distributed that power pretty evenly.

There are almost an infinite number of websites catering for the tastes of militaria collectors, be they focused on a specific area such as badges, or interested in the whole gamut of military collectables from uniforms through personal equipment to working vintage vehicles.

Taken in the Adur Valley in Sussex, this image shows a pillbox, typical of the kinds that were thrown up in haste during 1940. Notice that the entrance is at the front, beneath the machine-gun embrasure, to prevent an enemy sneaking up from behind. Anyone attempting to get inside also has to crawl, another protective method. Finally, notice the dog-leg blast wall to reduce the explosive effect of hand grenades being lobbed at the entrance.

Primarily aimed at the British collector I've included the following sites and resources that originate in the UK and which I have found most useful. Some are well known and some might not be very familiar, especially to the beginner. I hope cosmopolitan readers will forgive me for the bias in this brief review. It is not just solely based on my personal experience but is also dictated by the very real space limitations of a directory listing even a small percentage of the huge number of US, Canadian, Australian and European websites that service international collectors.

I'll start this survey with a look at a couple of famous militaria dealerships whose premises I used to visit regularly in the 1980s and early 1990s but which now maintain more of an online presence rather than a retail, shop-based one.

The late Tom Greenaway had been selling antique arms and armour since 1960, working from a stall layout in London's Portobello Road. In 1968 he opened his famous premises in Thayer Street, in London's prestigious Marylebone district, and in the early 1970s he was joined by his sons Phil and Chris. Sadly, Tom and Phil are no longer with us but Blunderbuss's militaria business carries on today through the efforts of Chris.

'Since we opened, and to the present day, we have seen the collecting of arms, armour and militaria change in many ways, from early morning street market dealing and in our shop face to face with the customer, to the current trend of selling by mail order and

Constructed from more than 5,000 bags of cement, this range-finding and navigation tower at Corbière was built by the German occupying forces during WWII and commands excellent views and covers the westward approaches to Jersey.

The tower was used until 2004 by Jersey Radio and as a marine transmitter for shipping. It has since been converted to holiday accommodation, appropriately restored in the German modernist Bauhaus style!

on the Internet,' says Chris on their current website (www.blunderbussantiques.co.uk), which, like their famous high-street business, is to be recommended. With a stock comprising everything from bayonets of all periods, antique weapons and militaria including flintlock pistols and long guns, First World War and Second World War items of every sort – including combat equipment, clothing, personal kit, paperwork, insignia, helmets, military knives, respirators, caps and boots, aviation and even naval items (but not much post-Second World War material) – Blunderbuss is a definite look-see for the British collector.

Founded by Malcolm Fisher and the late Simon Fisher, Regimentals is another long established London-based militaria dealership that manages an impressive website (www.regimentals.co.uk) and one I can heartily recommend to any collector.

Beginning to trade around the markets of the South of England in 1969, Simon Fisher quickly saw his business develop until he and Malcolm oversaw the growth of the company and its move into premises off Islington's Upper Street, where it remained for nearly fifteen years. Today successive generations of the Fisher dynasty manage and run Regimental's thriving business online. Covering a range of worldwide militaria from 1750 to the present day, with an especial focus on conflicts such as the Battle of Waterloo, Crimean, Boer and even Vietnam wars (First World War and Second World War items are a given stock) and specializations in RAF, SOE, Commando and US Airborne material, there's not much that the Fishers and their business partners don't know about military collectables.

Bob Tredwen's business, www.militaryantiques.co.uk, can trace its heritage back to Camden Passage in Islington and the lively antique markets held there on Wednesdays and Saturdays. His first shop was in the Mall Antiques Arcade and after five years he moved to a larger shop further along the Passage called Phelps Cottage. Local redevelopment work in the area saw Bob's physical retail presence decline and his mail order business increase as a consequence. Today he operates solely via the website and mail order.

M4A2 Sherman beach armoured recovery vehicle (BARV) pictured at the War & Peace Show, Beltring, Kent, in 2007. One of nearly 4,000 military vehicles in attendance at one of the largest military spectaculars in the world, the Sherman BARV was used on the D-Day invasion beaches to remove vehicles that had broken down or become swamped by the tides. Capable of operating in 9ft (2.7m) deep water, around sixty were deployed on the invasion beaches.

Nick Hall is a long-time acquaintance of mine. Familiar to collectors around the world, at the time of writing he had just sold his well-known south coast premises but was still looking for a purchaser for his business, Sabre Sales. Then, perhaps, he can realize his ambition of retiring.

Nick has been a collector of arms and armour since childhood and was considered so unique in the 1950s that he even featured in the BBC children's programme *All Your Own* and was interviewed about his hobby by Hew Weldon.

While serving in the Bermuda Police in the 1960s, Nick continued to collect antique arms and on his return to the United Kingdom in 1970 he joined a military collectors' society in the garrison town of Aldershot, Hampshire. Very soon he began to 'wheel and deal', as he put it, in the pursuit of his hobby and quickly gained a reputation as someone who could get hold of rare and valuable military collectables.

This marvellous WWI Bristol F.2b can be seen at the Shuttleworth Collection at Old Warden in Bedfordshire. An aircraft that first entered service in March 1917, the 'Brisfit' could be thrown around the sky with ease and was responsible for many kills during WWI. The aircraft remained in production until 1926. This machine, D8096, was built in 1918, too late to see service during WWI, being used by No. 208 Squadron in Turkey instead.

Militaria became such an important part of Nick's life that in September 1988 be took the plunge and decided to turn his hobby into a career and opened his shop, Sabre Sales, in Southsea, Hampshire. For twenty-five years Nick Hall's emporium quickly became a Mecca for collectors from all over Europe and it's hard to imagine the Portsmouth area without the larger-than-life presence of the 'legendary' Mr Hall.

Hardly believing that the world of military collectables faced the imminent loss of this inimitable character, I took the opportunity to ask Nick if he had any words of wisdom for the novice collector. Without hesitation he immediately boomed one of them, 'Specialization!' He then quickly went on to tell me that when he started out in the hobby he collected almost everything: suits of armour, matchlock muskets, flintlocks, pistols, you name it. Very soon he filled every room in his house. 'I couldn't live with it. Couldn't move. So I sold the lot,' he recalled. But you can't keep a good man down or, if you are a collector deep down like Nick was, break the habit of a lifetime. It wasn't long before Nick began collecting. But on this second serious venture he specialized and chose a very particular period: The British Empire 1880-1914.

Nick told me that the 1960s was a time when those who had actually administered the empire in the armed or civil services were dying off one by one. House clearances and

Volunteer policeman Steve George, PC 61, takes a break from the excitement of the War & Peace Show in Kent and enjoys a cup of Rosy Lee (tea) with Joanne Bayter and Sue Padgham.

siblings' sales of late relatives' possessions revealed a cornucopia of fantastic items from the colonies. It's hard to believe today, but Nick told me that he often acquired genuine Zulu shields for the equivalent of 25p! This 'happy time' didn't last long, however, and very soon things liked edged weapons and armour, especially, became too expensive for the average collector. So Nick specialized again, this time concentrating on uniforms. This presented its own challenges. Nick told me that the biggest obstacle was the activity of the venerable British moth. 'We breed the most voracious moths in the world,' he said, recalling that US customers in particular were very unhappy to discover dreaded limey 'woolly bears', the final stage between moults as the caterpillar outgrows its skin. North American moths are much more benign so you can appreciate US collectors being unhappy about this British immigrant. So specialization came at a cost, even for Nick Hall.

I asked Nick what were the main things for the novice collector to consider. Again, without any hesitation, his answer was straightforward and direct: 'Those items in best condition. Quality is always at a premium and things in the finest condition command the highest value. This is why I have never dealt in those so-called aviation relics, bits of twisted aluminium, which some enthusiasts spend an inordinate amount of time

With more than 1,000 stalls stretching across 30 acres, the War & Peace Show in Kent is a Mecca for militaria enthusiasts. One of the most popular venues for the display of vintage military vehicles, it is no surprise to see row upon row of classics such as these 'Trucks, 1/4 ton, 4 x 4', better known as the Jeep. These brilliant vehicles were manufactured on a 24/7 production line basis by both the originator, Willys, and under licence by Ford. Between 1941 and 1945, nearly half a million Willys MB and Ford GPW Jeeps were pressed into military service.

exhuming from the earth. If you buy something that is clean and in good condition and, if it is an item of clothing, of a good size, you can't go far wrong.' Nick told me that the same basic rules apply to those starting out in badge collecting. Quality is of paramount importance. If a badge has damaged lugs then it is worthless – especially if it is a post-war anodized badge manufactured in a material that can't be soldered (with care, the fittings of brass badges can be reattached). Nick was, however, quick to point out that anodized, or 'Staybrite', badges should not be discounted (for a long time 'serious' collectors shunned them). He reminded me that many post-Second World War regiments that are no longer with us or have been amalgamated with other formations, only ever had anodized badges and that many of these are now becoming quite rare. As regards things that are now becoming much sought after and well worth collecting, Nick said that almost anything to do with the RAF, from either Fighter or Bomber Commands, topped the list, closely followed by militaria associated with British, Commonwealth or US Second World War airborne forces. He told me that it was with some dismay that he had to admit that Third Reich militaria still attracted a disproportionate amount of attention. As a dealer of renown it was perhaps not surprising that Nick also stressed the importance of doing business with established concerns because they had reputations to protect; professional traders were more likely to be selling genuine items, he said.

Now that he was about to retire from the business with which he had been so closely associated for decades, I asked if he could tell me what his career highlights were: 'Appearing on *All Your Own* when aged only fourteen is still a favourite memory. I also did the costumes for *A Bridge Too Far* and *The Eagle Has Landed*, two films that came out around the same time and that both starred Michael Caine, though he served in rival armies in each movie.' Another career peak was when Sabre Sales was contracted to work on *Saving Private Ryan*, directed by Stephen Spielberg, and *Band of Brothers*, which was co-produced by Spielberg and Tom Hanks. In fact, Nick saw, first-hand, just how influential the Oscar-winning director is. Despite his describing what the dozens of authentic Second World War German ammo boxes loading down his vehicle were for after a foray in France, customs were having none of it. However, the mere mention that Sabre Sales was en route to deliver its bounty to a Spielberg location shoot resulted in the delivery being immediately waived through the frontier controls without further ado.

The Internet has made a huge difference to the traditional activities of all militaria dealerships and its effect on Sabre Sales is no different. Said Nick: 'The web has increased our market dramatically. Only the other day we sold a Royal Logistics Corps lady officer's mess dress, complete with jacket, skirt and bib, to a man in Taiwan! It's now a truly global market.' Nick pointed out that for dealers there is a down side to the online market: Instead of selling things to his shop, visitors often pop in for a free valuation and then, armed with an idea of its worth, sell it themselves on eBay or an equivalent.

Having sold his iconic premises in Castle Street, Nick was then in the process of 'a massive stock clearance as we "retreat" from one store to another.' Whatever the future of www.sabresales.co.uk Nick was hopeful that he would continue to be involved with it in some way in the future, at least as a consultant. 'Give me a mobile and because I'm creative and want to remain active, I'm sure I will still be involved in some way.' Cheers to that I hear those who are familiar with Nick saying; though just what his family think of an on-going relationship with khaki serge and 'Blancoed' webbing is another thing …

If you are unable to deal with dealers directly, either in person, online or on the phone, then the Internet has delivered a huge range of resources both as traditional websites that can be perused at leisure or in the form of forums, blogs and other locations that have proliferated amidst the recent explosion in social media.

One very useful British initiative is Milweb, which claims to be 'the world's largest and busiest military marketplace for Military Vehicles, Militaria and Deactivated Weapons'. The www.milweb.net site includes full listings of military vehicle events, militaria fairs and re-enactor/living history events as well as those for auctions and disposal sales (for surplus military equipment) and is used by more then 45,000 military collectors, enthusiasts and buyers each week.

Full of drawer after drawer of every kind of military collectable, Nick Hall's Sabre Sales is a veritable treasure trove for the enthusiast. This photo shows just one drawer of many that is packed with boxes of badges and insignia of every kind.

Another very interesting community, with a forum full of numerous interesting militaria-related topics divided into sub forums and threads and conversations between individual members, is the Gentlemen's Military Interest Club (www.gmic.co.uk). With subjects covering every conceivable interest from British and Commonwealth military to that of Germany, Russia, the USA – you name it – and including insignia, medals, military vehicles, campaigns, books and movies, this site appears to be just the ticket.

It's beyond the scope of this book to discuss online resources in detail. There are just too many and quite a few of them seem to fade and die just as quickly as they burst onto the Internet. One site that is always worth a look and is likely to be around as long as Britain thinks it is worth defending these isles is that of the British Army, and this book would be far from complete without mention of www.army.mod.uk. This location is a massive source of information and not just what you'd expect, such as advice on how to go about joining the Army, but also much more general stuff. It is a great resource to

Although they weren't armed and situated in the front line, women fought and won a vital battle in WWII. They prevented the Home Front from imploding by carrying on regardless. They didn't panic. Instead, they conjured up meals for the family from the most meagre ingredients. Serving dishes like those featuring snook, a fish unknown in the UK until WWII but well known in the US (three USN submarines have even been named after it) and meals like Woolton Pie, a nutritional meal despite the fact that it didn't contain any meat (Lord Woolton became Minister of Food in 1940), British housewives sustained the nation.

find out more about the structure of the British Army, its history, traditions and operational deployment. Highly recommended.

Another website to which I have referred on a regular basis is www.kellybadge.co.uk, a mail order business run by Ian Kelly since he left the Regular Army in 1990. Author of the regularly updated *Cloth Head-Dress Badges of the British Army* Ian is also a regular contributor to *The Armourer* magazine (see below).

There are numerous living history and military re-enactment events held annually throughout Britain. Not surprisingly considering the British weather, most of these take place in the summertime – whatever that is. Most of these outdoor events include a bevy of trade stands where enthusiasts can purchase sought-after items while they take a break from Cavaliers and Roundheads doing unspeakable things to each other in the events arena (see www.thesealedknot.org.uk) or US Long Range Reconnaissance Patrols (LRRPs) battling 'Charlie' in the A-Shau Valley in Vietnam (see www.101strangersvietnam. org.uk). Living history events provide the added bonus of providing something often spectacular to see as a supplement to frenetic haggling and bartering with dealers. Naturally, they are rather more appealing to friends and loved ones than simply being dragged around behind an enthusiast at standard military jumbles where the only entertainment is a ten-minute stop for a cup of tea and a bacon sandwich!

Probably one of the best days out for the militaria fan is a visit to the famous annual War & Peace Show in Kent. At the time of writing (late 2012) it has been announced that the show is leaving its famous home at the Beltring Hop Farm after a presence of twenty-five years. The latest event attracted 110,000 visitors. making it the world's biggest military vehicle enterprise. Produced in association with the Invicta Military Vehicle Preservation Society, Rex Cadman's massive show was set to move to a new home, RAF Westenhanger, at Folkestone Racecourse in Kent. Visit www.thewarand peacerevival.co.uk for more information.

Held each September since 1998, The Goodwood Revival is a three-day festival for fans of vintage vehicles and aeronautica located at the Goodwood Motor Circuit near Chichester in Sussex. This venue ranked alongside Silverstone as Britain's leading racing venue throughout its active years between 1948 and 1966. In the summer of 2010 the organizers launched a brand new concept in British festivals – 'Vintage at Goodwood' – providing an award-winning event for fans of British Cool and Popular Culture to fully indulge their love and passion for the golden era of British style and influence. You can't keep a good soldier or fighter pilot down, so don't be surprised to see many enthusiasts attending in full battledress or garbed in the rather more casual attire of the Home Guard or Civil Defence. Take a look at www.goodwood.co.uk/revival for more information.

Established by long-time collector Ian Durrant in 1995, Sentimental Journey is a specialist supplier of British militaria from the 1914–1965 period. Ian served in the Territorial Army for about nine years and in a mixture of units- Royal Artillery, HSF, Infantry and Royal Signals- and he knows his stuff. So much so that www.sentimental journey.co.uk is used by re-enactors, collectors, schools, teachers, theatrical dressers and property masters from the film industry on a regular basis.

A thriving and active community where badge collectors can exchange views, seek advice or seek out 'must haves' is the British Badge Forum (www.britishbadge forum.com), where material in the form of members' albums is accessible to actively-posting registered members. The albums hold large numbers of images of military insignia and form a considerable illustrated reference about the history of British and Commonwealth military insignia.

It is nearly twenty years since the *The Armourer* magazine was launched at Stockport Arms Fair in January 1994 and despite the economic ups and downs and changing buying habits of consumers, the owners, Warners Group, reckon the 'militaria collecting scene hasn't changed a great deal.' For more information visit www.warnersgroup.co.uk.

Skirmish magazine is the world's leading multi-period historical re-enactment and living history magazine. It is produced by a dedicated team for re-enactors, living

Re-enactors enjoy nothing better than arriving at an event in period costume and riding in an appropriate vintage vehicle. These 'US' soldiers obliged me with a very positive thumbs-up before they and their vehicle, an immaculately restored M3 half-track, entered the display arena at the War & Peace Show in 2007.

historians and history enthusiasts from around the world, and covers all periods in world history from the last 3,000 years. Have a look at www.skirmishmagazine.com for more information.

In recent years a couple of websites catering for those keen to search the military records of family members who served in the armed forces have come to more prominence. 'Ancestry' is one and 'Find My Past' is the other. Today, together with visits to traditional government sources such as The National Archives (www.archives.gov/veterans/military-service-records) enthusiasts can also search the military records at www.ancestry.co.uk/cs/uk/military or www.findmypast.co.uk, which started life in 1965 when a small group of leading professional genealogists and heir hunters formed what was then known as 'Title Research' and which in 2010 as 'Find My Past' merged with a number of other businesses that included Friends Reunited.

Auction houses can be useful resources for research and wonderful places to pick up a bargain if you've got the readies available. Catalogues and viewing days can provide an excellent supplement to one's knowledge about the precise look of a military antique. Simply seeing what the passage of time does to a military object – not to mention the ravages of active military service – provides the collector with the necessary to be able to distinguish a genuine from a fake item. There are many excellent auction houses in Britain but I think it worthwhile listing a few of those I think might prove most useful to the militaria collector.

Holding three regular sales each year in their fine Georgian country house on the Thames, Bosleys attract buyers from all over the world. Have a look at www.bosleys.co.uk to find out more. Similarly, Warwick and Warwick (www.warwickandwarwick.com) is a well-known and professional firm and one of Britain's foremost public auctioneers of medals and associated militaria. Established in 1928, Wallis and Wallis of Lewes, Sussex, is a particularly well-known auction house and holds frequent excellent sales of arms, armour and other militaria. Visit www.wallisandwallis.co.uk for more information. Staying in Sussex, auctioneers Toovey's (www.tooveys.com) are also particularly expert when it comes to military items and in recent years they can claim many successful sales of militaria.

Should you want a break from iPads and laptop monitors and want simply to sit down in an armchair to read something, then publications like *The Armourer* or *Skirmish*

I pass this pillbox every time I commute to London by train. It is quite close to the railway line a few miles north of Horley in Surrey. Hexagonal and of brick-built construction, it was proof against rifle fire and shell splinters. Part of the GHQ Line that swept around the southern half of London, this was one of the defences urgently constructed by the directorate of Fortifications and Works, set up at the War Office in May 1940 and led by Major General G.B.O. Taylor. Both the railway line and the nearby A23 would have been a main axis of advance if the Germans had chosen to land in Sussex. It is my favourite pillbox.

magazines already mentioned, or reference books such as those classic guides to British Army badges written by Kipling & King and May, Carmen & Tanner and R.J. Wilkinson-Latham, or Brian L. Davis's numerous works about Third Reich uniforms and insignia, provide an accessible and pleasant way to learn more about militaria. However, there's one often overlooked resource within reach of most of us. Like the Internet it is nominally 'free' but unlike most modern electronic media it only works if you get up and go outside. I am, of course, talking about visits to museums and national collections.

It's probably no surprise that the United Kingdom, a composite of quite different nations each crammed into very limited island acreage, each with rich military traditions, is the home for some of the best military collections in the world. Our island people always seemed to punch beyond their weight. As a seafaring bunch dependant on a strong military to guarantee their security and with a skill for exploration and acquisition to both provide raw materials and a commercial knack to provide wealth, at one time the British Empire was the largest in world history, covering around twenty-five per cent of the world's land surface. Several British museums go a long way to revealing how Britain's military delivered the conquests necessary to achieve such imperial success and how, for many years at least, they strove to ensure it remained inviolate. The first, which explores the activities of the British Army from its inception with the unification of England and Scotland into the Kingdom of Great Britain in 1707, is Chelsea's National Army Museum. A stone's throw from the fashionable King's Road, this is the perfect venue to see priceless and original uniforms and artefacts from conflicts ranging from the Napoleonic, Crimean, Zulu and Boer wars. It's First World War, Second World War, Korean War, Falklands Conflict, Gulf War and Afghanistan War exhibits are equally notable. Badge and medal collectors will have a field day and military vehicle enthusiasts will be surprised at just how much hardware is packed into this modern, well designed museum. A much larger number of military collectables can be studied at London's Imperial War Museum. Founded in 1917 to commemorate the First World War, which was still being fought, the collection was originally housed in the Crystal Palace at Sydenham Hill, where the museum opened to the public in 1920. In 1924 the museum moved to space in the Imperial Institute in South Kensington and finally in 1936 it acquired a permanent home at the former Bethlem Royal Hospital in Southwark (at one time the location of a notorious asylum from where the word 'Bedlam' is derived). The IWM's remit is the coverage of conflicts, especially those involving Britain and the Commonwealth, from the First World War to the present day. To facilitate this it comprises a family of five museums: IWM London; IWM North in Trafford, Greater Manchester; IWM Duxford, near Cambridge; the Churchill War Rooms in Whitehall, London, and the historic ship HMS *Belfast* moored on the Thames near Tower Bridge in London: Most militaria enthusiasts are especially drawn to the Land Warfare hall at Duxford – also a must-see for aviation fans as it is located on one of the RAF's most famous Battle of Britain period airfields. The hall is jam-packed with modern dioramas and numerous vehicles and field pieces that show men in context with the hardware with which they fought and the terrain they fought on. The Forgotten War exhibition highlights the political, military and personal aspects of the Second World War in the Far East, the Pacific and, in particular, Burma, between 1941 and 1945. Land Warfare is also home to the Royal Anglian Regiment Museum which deals with the history of the East and Royal Anglian Regiments since the amalgamations of the former County Regiments from 1958–1960. Also in London the RAF Museum at Hendon provides the chance to see an unrivalled collection of RAF aircraft, fighters, bombers and even the dirigibles of the Royal Engineers from whence the Royal Flying Corps and then the Royal Air Force developed. Naturally this large site, which comprises numerous exhibits displayed across a number of impressive buildings, is full of uniforms, insignia and equipment. A word of warning if you are planning your first visit: allow several hours and take your time as there's plenty to see. Before I finish my brief look at military collections in the capital I must mention the Royal Artillery Museum at Woolwich. 'Firepower' is housed in the historically secret Royal Arsenal and tells the history of artillery from slingshot to shell and from rocket to missile. Although there's plenty of impressively large guns to see there are also gunners' uniforms, personal possessions, artwork and medals. The dramatic centrepiece presentation 'Field of Fire' uses big screens and surround sound to tell the story of twentieth-century gunners from Burma to Bosnia in their own words.

South of London, both Kent and Hampshire are pretty well represented in the military museum stakes. Portsmouth and Chatham have long competed in the HMS *Victory* heritage stakes and whilst Portsmouth might be the current home of Nelson's historic flagship, Chatham can claim to be the place where it was actually built. Both the Historic Dockyards at Portsmouth and Chatham exhibit lots of rare and valuable militaria, some of it Napoleonic, of course, but most of it representing the activities of sailors and naval airmen throughout the numerous conflicts of the twentieth century. A small distance east of Portsmouth, Southsea is the home to the Royal Marines Museum. Staying in Hampshire, the Museum of Army Flying at Middle Wallop is the home for those interested in the airborne and the exploits of those brave soldiers of the Glider Pilot Regiment. Further west, Bovington in Dorset is home to the Tank Museum. Travel west a further 50 miles or so and you'll come to the Fleet Air Arm Museum at RNAS Yeovilton in Somerset. It should be noted that unlike those national collections such as the IWM, RAF and National Army Museums based in London, these provincial museums levy an entry fee.

Scotland is not short of fantastic military museums. One of my favourites is the Highlanders Museum at the spectacular Fort George in Inverness. This houses the unique collections of the Queen's Own Highlanders, Seaforth Highlanders, The Queen's Own Cameron Highlanders and Lovat Scouts. The National War Museum of Scotland at Edinburgh Castle explores the Scottish experience of war and military service over the last 400 years. Six galleries each focus on a different theme and include medals, uniforms, weapons, paintings, ceramics and silverware, all of which chart Scotland's

A collector from childhood, since the 1980s the 'legendary' Nick Hall has been the proprietor of Sabre Sales, the well-known militaria and costume hire dealership in Southsea, Portsmouth. At the time of writing, Nick had sold the famous premises in Castle Street and was looking for a buyer for his business. Nick plans to retire, his family being naturally reluctant to inherit bale upon bale of vintage khaki serge and yards of webbing, when as he says, he 'inevitably shuffles off this mortal coil.'

military history and the lives of many thousands of Scots.

England is home to numerous regimental collections. There are too many to mention here. I've visited quite a few but by no means all of them. Two of which spring to mind, however, and which I think are worthy of particular mention, are Fusiliers Museum of Northumberland at the Abbots Tower at Alnwick Castle and the DLI Museum & Durham Art Gallery at Aykley Heads, Durham. The DLI Museum is home to the treasures of the Durham Light Infantry, County Durham's own regiment, and charts the history of the DLI from 1758–1968 both through the eyes of the soldiers who fought and their families back home.

Visiting museums is a good way of seeing how best to display items such as badges, uniforms and military equipment. The science of display has developed exponentially since the days when objects were secured to peg boards in dusty, dimly-lit glass cabinets. And the days when curators thought it a good idea to cut and paste a typeset 'interpretation' graphic copied from the caption in a book onto a backing board are thankfully long gone.

It's not always obvious but a variety of historic military relics are dotted all around us and are not just to be studied by visits to museums and galleries. Dramatic evidence of Britain's rich military heritage can of course be seen in the numerous castles and fortified great houses that remain and are preserved as visitor attractions today. Equally impressive are surviving Thames Estuary army forts, which were constructed in 1942 to a design by Guy Maunsell, or the three stone Solent forts-Spitbank, Horse Sand and No Man's Land-built in the 1870s to protect the fleet anchorages in Portsmouth. However, I encourage the enthusiast to look around; military heritage can be seen everywhere, be it the thick concrete 'slab' that protected the Cabinet War Rooms in Whitehall or a humble sign for a community air raid shelter, which, despite all the odds, survives into the twenty-first century.

There's one Second World War British military relic that remains pretty ubiquitous – the good old pillbox. Fortunately, an organization exists that helps the beginner make sense of their design and purpose. It also assists in the interpretation of another legacy of the same period – the pyramidal concrete anti-tank obstacle known as 'dragon's teeth' to the enthusiast. 'Committed to the study and preservation of twentieth- century United Kingdom and international pillboxes and anti-invasion defences' is the promise on the website of the Pillbox Study Group (www.pillbox-study-group.org.uk), which first appeared on the scene as recently as June 2001. Since then this fine organization has chronicled the variety, purpose and building methods employed to construct a network that at one time consisted of a staggering 18,000 fixed defences, most of which were constructed during the invasion scare of 1940. Many of these breeze block, brick and concrete structures still exist, with farmers finding they provide useful dry storage. A visit to the Pillbox Study Group's site is an excellent way for the novice to gain an interpretation of these familiar architectural relics and discover just how important they would have been if Hitler had launched Operation Sealion.

It's all well and good dotting the landscape with fixed defences that await the invader on the surface and are ready to deter the easy advance of tracked vehicles, or by virtue of carefully aimed bursts of rifle or machine-gun fire thwart the progress of infantry. However, the advent of warfare from the air, the fall of bombs and especially the threat of gas being delivered by unstoppable bomber fleets, meant that an awful lot of Britain's military machines moved out of harm's way and went underground. It is well known that government operational centres were built deep below the surface ready for the authorities to retreat to if the cities above were, as many feared, reduced to rubble. In Second World War tunnel systems, like the 22 mile- (35km) series of prehistoric caves in Chislehurst in the south-eastern suburbs of London, were pressed into service. The Epsom Deep Shelter at Ashley Road, not too far from the famous racecourse, was built for use during the Second World War and has capacity for more then 1000 patients in bunks. Dug out of the chalk of the Epsom Downs, this shelter was one of the many built in anticipation of heavy casualties at the time of D-Day. The Cold War delivered a new threat: the prospect of a nuclear attack. The Royal Observer Corps (ROC) was tasked with forecasting nuclear attack and plotting the impact of warheads. To do so it's numerous sites were built underground and located throughout the British Isles. The end of the Cold War has removed the threat of the 'four-minute warning' and an imminent nuclear holocaust, and consequently the ROC's underground network has been decommissioned and the existence of surviving sites revealed.

Fortunately, there is a fantastic resource where enthusiasts can find out almost everything they need to know about Britain's once -secret underground military heritage. Founded in 1974, Subterranea Britannica is a UK-based society for all those interested in man-made and man-used underground structures. Usually known simply as 'Sub Brit', this very worthy organization has grown into a community of more then 1000 members. Visit www.subbrit.org.uk to discover facts about everything from Neolithic flint mines to nuclear bunkers.

Reading books, visiting collectors' fairs or participating in online forums to exchange views with other collectors will provide a massive amount of background knowledge to help the novice understand the history, development and, importantly, the context of individual military items. Visits to museums and galleries provide a fascinating supplement where surviving artefacts can be studied. Another really useful way of learning about military history and details about the numerous objects utilized in total war is to watch original period films or listen to preserved recordings and oral histories of those soldiers, sailors, airmen and civilians who experienced warfare first hand. Since its inception in 1917, when the British Cabinet decided that a National War Museum should be organized to collect and display material relating to the First World War, the Imperial War Museum has done just that – preserving not just objects but films and audio recordings which enable successive generations to greater understand past conflict and mankind's experience of it.

In the early 1920s the first custodian of this novel archive – the Government Cinematograph Adviser, Edward Foxen Cooper – developed procedures for the long-term storage and the preparation of film copies made specifically for preservation. The advent of the Second World War saw the museum's terms of reference enlarged to cover both world wars, and they were again extended in 1953 to include all military operations in which Britain or the Commonwealth have been involved since August 1914.

The collections of the Museum's Film and Video Archive now total some 20,000 hours and contain as much social, environmental, cultural and political history as it does military history and 'combat films'. A large proportion of material includes films from the British Armed Services and other UK public bodies such as major British documentaries like *Target for Tonight* (1941) and Oscar-winners like *The True Glory* (1945).

Significant amongst the museum's archive are the numerous films of the Crown Film Unit, an organization within the British Government's Ministry of Information during the Second World War. Formerly the GPO Film Unit, it became the Crown Film Unit in 1940. Its remit was to make films that appealed to the general public rather than the instructional kind of films that helped soldiers stay alive on the battlefield. The Crown Film Unit continued to produce films as part of the Central Office of Information (COI) until it was disbanded in 1952.

The IWM archive is crammed with fascinating films, many of which can be quite reasonably purchased on DVD. Amongst the many useful movies available, I can't recommend highly enough the work of film-makers like Humphrey Jennings. Not only was he one of the founders of the Mass Observation organization in 1954, but was hailed by fellow director Lindsay Anderson as 'the only real poet that British cinema has yet produced'. Anthony Asquith is another notable director who contributed to the film records we use as valuable reference today. To militaria buffs he is most famous for making *The Way to the Stars* in 1945. Another luminary is Harry Watt, who made *Target for Tonight* (mentioned above) as well as *The Foreman Went to France* which starred comedian Tommy Trinder.

Commercial organizations have also massively added to the film and audio evidence that students of military history can study today to better appreciate military history.

In my opinion, still the best documentary series about the Second World War is *The World at War*, the twenty-six-episode British television series made by Thames Television in 1973. Costing nearly £1 millionto produce, it was the most expensive television series ever. Creator Jeremy Isaacs used this money wisely, however, and from the sublime narration by Laurence Olivier to Carl Davis's stunningly evocative music the entire production shouted quality of the highest.

Whilst there have not been any historically accurate series of a similar magnitude to compare with *The Word At War* in the last forty years, there have been one or two edited compilations of rare Second World War colour footage that are worth watching. Two names worth mentioning are Jean-Louis Guillard and Henri de Turenne, while Isabelle Clarke's colourized *Apocalypse* not only brings lots or rare, much of it French, Second World War movie footage to life, it is also accompanied by an excellent and concise script. It is a very useful way for the novice to understand the contextual relationship of the inter-related strategies and individual campaigns of the Second World War.

In recent years even works of fiction, war movies such as *Saving Private Ryan* or docudramas like *Band of Brothers* and *The Pacific* have provided a useful and accurate addition to the enthusiasts' archives. In each of these productions attention to detail and historical accuracy was paramount. Actors were even sent on week-long military 'boot camps' so they could look and behave like soldiers in combat.

This sort of accuracy wasn't always the case, of course, and those of my generation though brought up on a steady stream of Hollywood blockbusting war movies soon realized what we were watching wasn't bang-on accurate. Before the days of CGI filmmakers were forced to use real objects, tanks and aircraft that worked. The exigencies of film-making, pressure from production accountants and limitations of a finite shooting schedule and props budget meant that on many, many occasions liberties were taken as far as accuracy is concerned. It's interesting to take a brief look at some of the movie cock-ups endured by film-goers of the so-called 'baby boom' generation!

I guess *The Dambusters*, starring Richard Todd, was the first war movie I really remember watching with the detailed focus of the budding military enthusiast (I'd read a lot by then, including Paul Brickhill's seminal 1951 book on which the film was based). This movie was made in 1954, five years before I was born, so I enjoyed it on TV and at the occasional Saturday matinee as I was growing up. I've seen it many times since, of course, and, apart from the same truly dreadful matter used repeatedly to suggest torrents of water shooting skywards as a result of successive bouncing bombs exploding, I think it is great.

Amazingly, when the movie was released the bouncing bomb, code-named 'Upkeep', was still on the Official Secrets List and as many fans know, some of the real test footage showing Wellington and Lancaster bombers practising with the weapon features heavily censored details of the bomb and the novel mechanism that Barnes Wallis invented to impart backspin and cause the 'munition to hop and skip across the water's surfaces. Additionally, the only test footage over a British dam actually showed aircraft releasing 'Highball', the smaller version of Wallis's bomb designed for use against enemy shipping.

Another historical inaccuracy in the film concerns the claim that, following a visit to the theatre, 617 Squadron's CO Guy Gibson, the leader of Operation Chastise, the raid on the Ruhr dams, came up with the novel method of using triangulated spotlights to help fix the height of the Lancaster bombers to 60 feet in the final run-up to the target. Actually, the idea belonged to Benjamin Lockspeiser, who as Chief Scientist at the Ministry of Supply came up with the idea during the First World War!

Much to my infantryman father's disappointment, back when I first watched *The Dambusters* I was a bit of an RAF fanatic. So I studied the Avro Lancasters shown on celluloid carefully and noticed that the aircraft each carried two 5in guns in the rear

Following a theme helps the collector to focus and concentrate both time and money to best effect. This selection of Royal Navy insignia is positioned next to some relevant WWII HMSO publications, which are still relatively easy to locate. HM *Corvette*, a 1942 novel by Nicholas Monsarrat, who famously wrote *The Cruel Sea* a decade later, and an August 1943 edition of *The Navy* is also included. Moving down from the top of the photograph, the various naval cloth badges can be identified as thus: petty officer (crown and crossed anchor); leading seaman (anchor); good conduct stripes; cap badge (rating class II); gunnery (crossed guns); leading torpedo man; torpedo man; signaller (winged lightning); visual signaller (flags); sail maker; PTI; stoker (3 props); airframe mechanic (4 props); motor mechanic (2 props); supply branch ('S' senior rate with crown); diver and bugler.

Collectors of Trench Art shouldn't solely limit their searches to objects from the 1914-18 period as this fine example from the Second World War demonstrates. Adolf Hitler formed the Afrika Korps on 11 January 1941 and on February 12th 1941 the Fuhrer's favourite General, Erwin Rommel was its commander and immediately despatched to Libya to take control. This shell case was decorated in 1941 when it seemed that the invincible Afrika Korps was unstoppable, have reversed the defeats suffered by its Italian ally, recapturing Libya and even threatening Egypt and the Suez Canal.

turrets, when, of course, they should have sported four .303in Browning machine guns! Tut, tut.

It's got to be admitted, however, that considering when it was made, *The Dambusters* isn't that bad and is mostly accurate (anyway, I realize that such productions aren't made to purely to satisfy military buffs) but what came a decade later should have been much better, when in fact as far as accuracy was concerned, war films from the 1960s certainly took liberties with exactitude – and I'm not just talking about the haircuts.

To the military enthusiast I reckon the most noticeable error in war films from the swinging sixties concerns the ubiquitous use of American M48 'Patton' tanks standing in for Second World War German heavy armour with M-3 half-tracks in place of the Wehrmacht's distinctive but quite different Hanomag Sdkfz 251 series of semi-tracked vehicles. One of my favourite films from this period was *Kelly's Heroes,* starring Clint Eastwood, Telly Savalas and Donald Sutherland. Fans of military history, like me, were very disappointed to see British Centurion and Russian T34/85s standing in for German Tiger tanks … Now I realize that being on the losing side meant most original Second World War German armour was destroyed and what survived ended up in the museums but, come on SFX men, what about a little ingenuity and some bent plywood? Until United Artists' *Battle of Britain* was released at the end of the decade and raised the bar for accuracy as far as the depiction of Second World War aircraft in war films was concerned, Hollywood didn't seem to worry too much about warplanes either. Though quite different from their later, fighter plane successor Messerschmitt, Me 108s doubled as Me 109s in *Von Ryan's Express,* the 1965 adventure drama starring Frank Sinatra that told of a group of Allied prisoners escaping from occupied Italy by hijacking a freight train and fleeing to neutral Switzerland. The 1968 movie *Where Eagles Dare* was even worse. Set in early 1944 and telling the story of eight Allied agents parachuted into a mountainous region of wartime Germany to rescue an American general before the Nazis can force him to reveal secret D-Day plans, it actually showed the Germans using Bell 47 helicopters in the castle where the captor was held! Despite the fact it is unlikely they

During the Great War life for the infantryman in the trenches was characterised by long periods of discomfort and boredom punctuated by moments of abject terror. Soldiers filled hours of inactivity by writing letters home or making keepsakes to send to loved ones. Many of these items, known as 'Trench Art' were fashioned using the detritus of war. Spent shell cases were abundant and Tommy Atkins soon became adept at making all manner of souvenirs from inert ammunition.

The scimitar, or 'pirate sword', shape seems to have been a terribly fashionable design for paper knives. This one features a handle constructed from sections sliced through .303 cartridges. I believe the black ring denotes an 'observing bullet', designed to break up with a puff of smoke on impact and the red ring, the more common, tracer round.

The simple peaked cap shown here is sealed by a 1900 One Penny with Queen Victoria's portrait on the reverse.

This ornately decorated Hotchkiss 37mm calibre 'Pom Pom' shell was manufactured by Pinchart Denys in Paris and features the added embellishment of a Royal Artillery badge.

would have been using such enemy equipment, even if the German forces had wanted one, they would have had to wait until 1946, when Bell manufactured the helicopter, before they could get hold of one. My final, and particularly picky error, comes from 1967 movie *The Dirty Dozen* which starred Lee Marvin, Ernest Borgnine and Charles Bronson and was about a dozen convicted murderers assigned to a do-or-die mission to assassinate German officers. During one scene set in an ambulance, a German doctor tells convicted commando 'Jefferson' played by Jim Brown: 'You're wearing Air Force insignia.' The US Air Force didn't exist until 1947 before that it was, of course, merely an air corps, a coequal to the Army Ground Forces, and remained one of the Army's combat arms, like the infantry.

Formed as a result of the merger of Vickers Limited and Sir W G Armstrong Whitworth & Company in 1927, Vickers Armstrong was one of Britain's largest arms manufacturers making field guns at Elswick and building ships nearby on the River Tyne. Large enough to be able to organise its own civil defence establishment, Vickers boasted Home Guard and ARP detachments The 1st battalion Vickers Armstrong Home Guard patrolled the company's vital shipyards on the Tyne and Vicker's ARP volunteers manned fire watching duties and acted as wardens in the event of incendiaries or high explosives starting conflagrations. Both these badges are manufactured from silver and exhibit striking art deco features.

But, please, don't let me put you off your viewing enjoyment. Above all else, Hollywood is about entertainment, and novels, on which most movies are based, are works of fiction, so we shouldn't get too hung up. Anyway, the novice military enthusiast starting out on the hobby is today spoilt with major productions being much more faithful to historical accuracy. One way they can do this, certainly as far as hardware is concerned, is by employing the plethora of digital techniques available in suites of CGI equipment. Now,at last, First World War aircraft can be conjured up; some, like those in Tony Bill's 2006 epic *Flyboys* and Nikolai Müllerschön's 2008 film *The Red Baron* (*Der Rote Baron*) are particularly well crafted. Stephen Spielberg's *Saving Private Ryan* and *Band of Brothers,* which he co-produced, are particularly accurate. Based on Stephen Ambrose's classic book, the latter was ground-breakingly accurate. However, even *Band of Brothers* featured an error apparent to some militaria fans. When the 101st Airborne was sent into Belgium just before the Battle of the Bulge they were ordered to remove the Screaming Eagle patch from their uniforms so the Germans would not know they were facing an elite division. Despite this the actors are seen wearing the emblem throughout their service in Europe!

In WW2 concerns about inflaming sectarian violence and giving weapons to potential republicans meant that the British government was not prepared to arm the civilian population in Northern Ireland as it did with the Home Guard on the mainland. In Ulster there was no Territorial Army and the Ulster Home Guard was administered through the Royal Ulster Constabulary and its members were sworn in as Special Constables. Not technically part of the armed forces of the Crown, members of the Ulster HG were not protected by the Geneva Convention and likely to be shots as guerrillas if Nazis made landfall in the six counties. In 1942 members of the Ulster Home Guard were re-attested as members of the British armed forces but still also wore the Royal Ulster Constabulary cap badge. 26,000 men volunteered to join the UHG, patrolling possible landing beaches and the border with the Republic of Ireland to prevent German spies attempting to infiltrate Ulster. Later in the war the Home Guard manned the anti-aircraft guns at Holywood and Londonderry. The UHG was disbanded in December 1944.

To prevent things spinning out of control, as mentioned at the beginning of this chapter, it is important to stay foussed and fixed on a precise goal. It makes sense to decide on a theme for your collection. Rather than simply collecting 'anything to do with the army' it would be more enjoyable and affordable to perhaps concentrate on a single regiment or, broader but still manageable, a service arm such as the REME (Royal Electrical and Mechanical Engineers), Army Air Corps or the RAF Regiment. Equally, perhaps you might just concentrate on a single time period (the First or Second world wars or Korean War, etc.) or on individual campaigns such as the emergency in Malaya in the 1950s, conflicts at Suez in late 1956 or the battle for the Falklands in 1982.

There are also numerous fascinating areas of military collectables on the periphery of traditional territories, such as badge and uniform collecting, and we have already seen the variety of items within what is probably the fastest growing of these at the moment – Home Front collectables. I recently sold a couple of dozen Second World War ARP, CD, Police and Auxiliary Fire Brigade helmets to a collector in Hong Kong and received the highest prices for such items, so I'm in a position to testify that not everyone is looking for decal emblazoned Second World War German Stahlhelms or 'Arnhem period' British paratrooper helmets.

Most objects are collected by enthusiasts who have a particular interest in a subject or period. Phil Collins is drawn to collectables associated with the Battle of the Alamo, which took place in Texas during the spring of 1836. Lots of other militaria fans, myself included, became fascinated with Second World War flying gear and army badges and equipment by watching classic 1960s' films like *633 Squadron*, *The Battle of Britain*, *The Longest Day and Zulu*. We delight in being able to actually own fighter pilot wings, a Royal Tank Regiment beret or even a set of Slade Wallis Webbing belonging to a nineteenth-century trooper of the 24th Foot. These items brought history to life and were coveted more for what they represented than any inherent financial investment. But it has to be admitted that if you have an eye for investment, collecting vintage militaria is probably a surer way of seeing your money grow than locking it away on deposit or trusting it to the vagaries of the stock market. Things in short supply increase in value at an exponential rate. Common items like 1937 Pattern British webbing or post war RAF Aertex flying helmets now command the highest prices. Genuine First World War items have long been popular and expensive. The forthcoming centenary of the outbreak of the conflict has pushed prices even higher. The death in 2009 of Harry Patch, the 'Last Fighting Tommy' who achieved the ripe old age of age of precisely 111 years and thirty-eight days, had already led to a rapid increase in the prices of items. Even quite common medals such as 'Pip, Squeak and Wilfred' (the affectionate names given to the three First World War campaign medals), the 1914 Star or 1914–15 Star, British War Medal and Victory Medal respectively are now achieving top prices. In total nearly 6,500,000 British war medals were awarded but of these only 110,000, the rarest, were struck in bronze. These were mostly issued to men from China, Malta and India serving in labour battalions

In December 2008 a set of three medals belonging to the famous war poet Captain Siegfried Sassoon sold for £4,375.00. You see, provenance is everything. Not surprisingly, anything that can be linked to a celebrity, especially one, who like Sassoon, Robert Graves, Wilfred Owen or Rupert Brooke, served on the front line, will command premium prices. However, such is the distance from both world wars that in 1990, when *A Nation Alone* the author's illustrated history commemorating the fiftieth anniversary of the Battle of Britain was published (at the time of writing the seventy-fifth anniversary is fast approaching and very few of those who served in the air or on the ground in Fighter Command in 1940 remain with us) so overwhelming is the appetite amongst collectors for almost anything that saw active service during the two conflicts, that prices continue to go up and up. Quality will out, however, and it has to be said that only the very best items will achieve top prices. So, as with almost anything, try to go for the best. Again, go for quality not quantity. However, and I must stress this, don't spend what you can't afford to be without. Collecting is a hobby; the dictionary definition is 'a leisure time activity pursued for pleasure'. There's no pleasure in having the best collection of German Second World War militaria (still the sector commanding the highest prices) if you've had to go without decent meals or live in an unheated home to achieve such success.

I touched on display in an earlier chapter, but it's worth repeating here that unless you are collecting purely for investment and have no real desire to enjoy the results of your labours, then you will want to put things on display (showing off your collection so that others can enjoy it also deters people from assuming you are a sad and lonely hoarder!). And again, try to invest in the best way of exhibiting your collection. So whether you arrange your treasures in an Art Deco walnut display cabinet with glazed doors and glass shelves, a painted antique shop display cabinet with twin-arched glass front and glazed doors, or a stunningly modern German or Italian system with asymmetrical shapes to the shelvess which doubles as a striking and functional room divider, give some thought to this oft-overlooked but important aspect of the hobby.

Index